Contemplative Meditation:

How to Build a Sustainable Daily Practice

Yuichi Handa, PhD

Book Layout ©2017 BookDesignTemplates.com
Cover Design by Islam Farid
Editing by Kim Derby
Illustrations by Jeff Rivard

Contemplative Meditation: How to Build a Sustain-
able Daily Practice/ Yuichi Handa. -- 1st ed.
Printed in the United States of America
ISBN 13:978-0692929926

Table of Contents

Preface

I'm sometimes asked why I meditate as much as I do. There are many reasons, but I think it comes down to one simple thing: love.

Not love as in meditating helps me to be a more loving person, although that's part of it. More than that, it's that the act of meditating is *about* love, like spending time with one's love and lover. If we had our way, wouldn't most of us want to spend at least a few hours each day, if not the entire day, with our love?

That's what meditation practice has become for me. It's like *coming home* to a love.

And yet, such relationships don't come about without effort, without their challenges, especially once past the "honeymoon" phase. Even the best relationships can feel painful and difficult at times. But through the process of coming home, again and again, to the same love, something wondrous begins to happen. We begin to find an inner well-spring of promise, joy, settledness, openness, and ultimately, love. And as we continue, we grow into this relationship, deeper and deeper.

Establishing a daily meditation practice is a way of creating such a relationship with the phenomenal world. It takes time and effort, but it's a wholly worthwhile endeavor. In these pages, I hope that you will find the promise of something meaningful and extraordinary, something that will become your way of coming back home to yourself, just as I have found it to be for myself.

Yuichi Handa

Chapter 1: Introduction

The intent behind this book is to help you to build a daily meditation practice, or what might be called a "formal" practice. It's been my experience as well as the experience of others whom I have helped in this regard that upholding and maintaining a consistent daily practice requires certain pieces to be in place. What I hope to convey in this book are those particular pieces and how they come together to form a robust and sustaining daily practice.

But before proceeding any further, I would like to pose a question to you: *What is your motivation for reading this book? Assuming that you are interested in having a daily meditation practice, why do you want it?*

Set the book down for a moment to reflect on this question.

A motivation for reading this book

I am assuming that part of your motivation for picking up this book is that you have an interest in meditation. Maybe you've tried it a handful of times to great benefit? Or maybe you've even been a meditator for many years, but somehow, the *daily* part of the practice has eluded you and your efforts?

When I ask people *why* they would be interested in having a daily meditation practice, the most common responses I hear are these:

- My life is so much better when I meditate regularly.
- I feel so wonderful and centered when I meditate!
- I enjoy the calm and peace of meditation, and it would be wonderful to have that as a daily part of my life.
- I need it!
- It helps me to overcome my anger.

- I like or believe in the philosophy of Buddhism, and I read in a book that it's important to meditate regularly.

Here, I want to point to motivation, or intention, and in particular, how one can modify or extend one's intentions, starting with an example from my own life: When I was about 20 years old, I had a mentor figure who was pivotal in my development as a young man. I respected him and held him in the highest esteem. But one day, he said something that upset me deeply (truth be told, I can't even recall what it was anymore). When I thought about his words, I began to nurse a resentment against him, to the point that I decided I was going to give him a piece of my mind.

I set out in my car to drive over to his place. My motivation, although not particularly conscious at the time, was to express my grievances and possibly to cast blame upon him.

As it turns out, he was outside mowing his front lawn as I approached. I parked about 100 yards from his house and began my walk toward him, filled with self-righteous hurt and bitterness. Yet, as I began walking toward the sight of him mowing his lawn, something in me began shifting. It was almost as if there were a tangible air of soft, gentleness about his being. And that quality about him began to open something in me. In turn, I started remembering the many ways he had helped and loved me as a young adult. As I continued watching him pushing the lawnmower, oblivious to my approach and to the emotional drama happening within my mind and heart, I felt myself becoming transformed. By the time I was close enough for him to notice me, I was free of my bitterness and felt only overflowing gratitude along with some embarrassment.

Later, when he was done with his lawn, we sat down to talk where I sheepishly shared with him the drama I had undergone, to which he burst out laughing.

In this example, my original intention of verbally attacking him was replaced or modified by an intention of openness and gratitude, to the extent that I ultimately chose to express my deepest appreciation for who he was and for his presence in my life. In this instance, my original motivation changed.

In other cases, we can bring two different motivations or intentions together. For example, when you go shopping at the grocery store and someone asks you why you go shopping, you might reply, *to buy food for the week*. But then maybe you're listening to the radio on the way to the store, and you hear something about how many people are depressed or lonely or on anti-anxiety medications. Suddenly, you start thinking that maybe half the people you run into at the grocery store are lonely, so instead of simply thinking about getting food, maybe you think about trying to brighten up someone's day by saying

hello. Or asking the cashier how their day is going. Or offering someone a heartfelt compliment or
expression of appreciation.

I think of this as a case where you maintain the original intention of obtaining food. But you also are en-
folding a new motivation in with the original
one. You still go to get groceries, but you bring in
another intention, that of brightening up someone
else's day. These aren't incompatible motivations, as
you can hold both at the same time.

Motivations can also be *extended*. To use the example of grocery shopping, maybe the original intention
is to buy food at the store. But if you think about
it—and let's say you have a family—then grocery
shopping is about buying food for your family, feeding your loved ones. Or if like me, you don't have a
family, then buying food is about nurturing a healthy
body, or ultimately, about being healthy. In this way,
one can *consciously* extend an original intention—
not just buying food, but buying it to support a
happy, healthy family or self.

Going back to the question I posed to you, think back
upon why you're reading this book. Whatever your
original motivation, I want to encourage you *right
now* to extend it. Or to enfold another intention into
it.

Maybe your original intention was simply to learn
more about meditation and how to make it a daily

thing. And maybe, added to that, there was the motivation of wanting to have more peace in your life. What I want to suggest is that you extend that motivation—not replace it—but extend it in the following manner, for example: *I want to meditate regularly—daily if possible—so that I can become more awake, clear, and open. And by being that much more awake, clear, and open, I can be more helpful to others.*

You're fusing an altruistic motivation *in* with your original one. You still may want to learn about meditation, which is a beautiful and noble intention, but you can also extend it to include others. In my experience, this blesses any undertaking and makes it much more powerful in effecting personal transformation. You're no longer motivated simply by personal welfare; you're including others in your journey.

I want to suggest that you pause here to see if you can extend your original motivation, if you haven't already.

If the idea of joining and extending your motivation feels abstract, an alternative is to make a prayer along the same lines, if you happen to be open to that. If not, that's fine also. I'm simply offering it as an alternative to the notion of modifying and extending one's intentions.

Here's an example of a prayer you might try: *Please bless my act of reading this book, so that I can become more awake and open, and as a result, I may be of greater benefit and help to others.* Such a prayer, I believe, resets our intentions so that whatever endeavor we're about to undertake is no longer just about ourselves. It begins to *consciously* include others.

This can be a meaningful way to start any "spiritual" activity, and I hope you'll consider it as such. I will say more about setting these types of intentions in a later chapter. For now, please consider checking in with your motivations and modifying/extending them as explained above each time you sit down to read this book.

The organization of this book

This book is organized into three sections: The first section (chapters 1 – 4) covers preliminary information that will act as a set-up to the heart of the book, sections two and three. In the second section (chapters 5 - 9), I lay out what I consider to be vital and necessary aspects of a robust and consistent meditation practice. In the third (chapters 10 – 18), I introduce analytic or contemplative meditation and continue with an exploration of the contemplation of impermanence and death.

A key feature of the second and third sections is that I offer you, the reader, a weekly plan for slowly setting up your daily practice. I offer suggestions that go from week to week. The "course," if you want to think of it as such, runs for twelve weeks.

My suggestion is that upon reading each weekly section, that you either close the book for the ensuing week, or simply re-read what you've read up until that point for the week. Try not to skip ahead. Once the week has passed, pick up where you left off, read the next section and pause for another week. And so on. The reason behind this suggestion of not getting ahead of things will be made clear in the next chapter that you read.

In summary, if your goal is to garner as much information as possible about how to set up a daily practice, feel free to disregard the suggestion of taking your time through this book. But, if your goal is to set up your own daily practice—in other words, you're more interested in the actual outcome as opposed to information gathering—I hope that you'll focus less on the reading, and more on the doing.

Chapter 2: Touch the floss box

Building a daily meditation practice amounts to creating a new habit, which is the same as implementing change, but not just any change, but the kind that is sustainable in nature. In line with this goal, there is an approach to change that comes from Japan called *kaizen*. The character for *kai-* means change and -*zen* means happiness or goodness, so it is literally "good change." But its meaning is more a sense of continuous, long-term, incremental change.[1]

I want to give two examples of the application of *kaizen*—one of which is systemic, and the other, personal.

---

[1] There are many excellent books that focus exclusively on *kaizen*, such as Robert Mauer's *One Small Step Can Change Your Life: The Kaizen Way* and Masaaki Imai's *Kaizen: The Key to Japan's Competitive Success*.

About thirty to forty years ago in Japan, educators and other involved parties saw the need for reform-like change in their educational system. Some of you may know that the United States has a long history of trying to reform education also. What you may not know, unless you're an educator yourself, is that in the US, the tendency has been to make one *revolutionary* change, over and over again, to little avail. This doesn't work for deep systemic and cultural reasons.[2]

And yet in Japan, they've actually reformed the way teaching is done. They started with a vision for where they wanted to be in 20 years. From there, they asked the question, *What do we need to do now and in the next year, to get us to where we want to be in 20 years?* And that's what they set about to do and have since accomplished and continue to accomplish to ever greater degrees.

Although I've just short-thrifted a much more complex process, it's a nutshell version of how educators in Japan laid out a plan to incrementally change how teaching looks in Japan.

A personal example from my own life may be more relatable. It starts with the fact that I've never liked flossing, and in fact, I resisted it for most of my

---

[2] See Stigler & Hiebert's *The Teaching Gap* for a more in-depth analysis of educational reform in the US and in Japan.

life. Up until a few years ago, I flossed only the day before a dental exam and then for two or three days afterwards. Then maybe once a month after that, just to see how much my gums would bleed. I even bought a Waterpik—one of those electric machines that pumps water at a high velocity in-between your teeth—which was fun for about a month but then got boring, and then, forgotten.

One day I decided to apply the approach of *kaizen* to flossing. My ultimate goal was to floss daily. I figured that if I was flossing daily in six months, I would be happy. Then I asked myself *what I would need to do for the first week* to move closer to my ultimate goal of daily flossing.

What I decided upon was that for the first week, my only commitment was to *touch* the floss box. It was hard at first (believe it or not). My floss box was usually buried under a heap of other bathroom junk, and I usually didn't even see it for weeks, even months at a time. So I had to dig it out from underneath the rubble of other stuff I rarely used.

To make my job easier, I placed the floss box by itself, right next to the bathroom sink (which didn't look aesthetically pleasing), so that I wouldn't forget about my commitment, but also, so that it would require the least amount of effort on my part to reach out and touch it. I could basically graze it when bending down to wash my face or when reaching for the toothbrush nearby.

After the first few days, this became easy.

My next step (the next week) was to pull out a piece of floss and throw it away. While this felt wasteful, I wanted to stay faithful to the idea of *incremental change*. I didn't want to overwhelm myself with an onerous level of commitment yet. The long-term goal was already set, and there was no hurry for me to arrive there any earlier than I had originally envisioned. The idea was that *I wanted each step to feel easy,* not like major change or work.

Then the next week, I flossed just one tooth, (or one space, that is), and into the trash the string went! From there, I went to two teeth. Mind you, I spent a full week on each phase/stage. *It took just as much discipline in holding myself back from flossing more as it did in showing up for the actual flossing.* This is important, and I will say more about it later, but *not moving ahead of schedule was the key discipline.* Had I flossed my entire mouth on a day I was feeling particularly motivated, it likely would have set up some subconscious or conscious expectation that I could do it again, or that I *should* do it again. And of course, that would likely have deterred me from flossing my teeth at all the next day, or some other future day.

So an important point in the process of *kaizen* is having a slow plan and sticking to it—that is, not getting behind *or* ahead of it.

Once I got to two teeth, I felt that jumping to just the middle five to six spaces on the top and bottom wasn't much of a stretch, so I focused on that for a month. Yes, an entire month. It felt like such a jump to be doing the middle ten to twelve spaces from just two spaces that I wanted to give it a full month for it to feel like a stabilized habit. But I also chose the middle teeth because they were the easiest and most fun for me! I was getting over ten spaces flossed, and it still didn't feel burdensome.

The next month I added one of the quadrants (e.g., top-right, top-left, bottom-right, or bottom-left). Again, I was very disciplined about stopping after doing just one quadrant. Even if I felt like doing another quadrant, I stopped myself. Naturally, I switched off on the quadrants from day to day, but I wasn't being particularly systematic about this, so I likely over-flossed some quadrants while neglecting others. This wasn't a big deal to me since I was just happy to be flossing at all!

In the ensuing months, I added an additional quadrant each month until I was doing my entire mouth each day. I'm happy to say, I've now made a sustaining habit of flossing all of my teeth daily! I've even gotten to the point of wanting to do it twice or three times a day on occasion, but that's another story altogether.

And by the way, I do brush my teeth twice a day.

When you build a practice slowly, it's not as intimidating. This is the kind of attitude and approach I would like to suggest in meditation. Easy and slow, but steady and sustaining.

For those of you who already meditate nearly every day and have been doing so for a long time, the pace that I set might be a bit slow for you, so you might just tweak the times to suit your purposes. Again, I want to reiterate that the long-term goal is to set a *daily* practice, specifically, a 21-minute daily practice, in 12 weeks. If you're a bit 'unusual' like me, then you might work your way up to a few hours a day. But that isn't necessary. (I've been doing this for a long time.)

When we get to the second section of this book, we'll set a modest first-week goal, one that you feel you can commit to, and then keep expanding across time. It'll be similar to touching the floss box. From there, we'll fill in the pieces so that by the end of 12 weeks, you'll have a fully fledged meditation practice!

I've taken it as a given that you the reader are interested in building or inhabiting a daily meditation practice. But just in case you started reading this book because you accidentally bought this book thinking it was something else, or you're being forced to by your therapist, partner, parent, professor, friend, or inner demon voice into reading this, I hope it will prove useful if I briefly share why I find having a daily practice to be useful, helpful, and worthwhile.

For me, having a regular practice is a bit like have an anchor in my life, or an oasis or a foundation. It's the foundation that allows me the possibility of doing practices such as straightforward mindfulness meditation, introspection and inquiry, energetic work, visualization exercises, even personal writing, as well as the more esoteric Tibetan meditation practices that I engage in—that can transform who I am, both my heart and mind. If I didn't have such a foundation to return to, I can't imagine being able to engage in these other challenging practices. And without the possibility of transformation, I'd either be very stuck in my life (which sometimes happens anyways), or be entirely dependent upon someone else to get me out of my rut. In this way, having a daily practice offers me a vital and robust path toward greater self-reliance as well as personal transformation and growth. These qualities then afford me the capacity to connect with others on a more intimate and meaningful basis, allowing me some level of fulfilment but also ample opportunities to support others in their growth and meaning-making in this life.

It's for these reasons and many more that I value my meditation practice.

But now, I'll not be going further into the merits of meditation in this book. Instead, I would like to maintain a one-pointed focus, which is to support you in building a daily practice. There are many books and resources on the value and merits of meditation. I imagine that most of you have read or are familiar with them.[3]

Before carrying on any further, I'd like to share just a bit more about my own relationship to practice, to help emphasize the importance of continuous, incremental change.

I started meditating about 30 years ago. I was a freshman in college, lived in the dorms at NYU, and I would go into my closet for about an hour every night in an attempt to sit quietly. I didn't really know what I was doing. I would just try. Then a few months later, I went to a Zen group in the city and learned how to sit. And that's how I began.

---

[3] If not, you can easily search for a good book on amazon.com. In particular, I recommend Jack Kornfield's *A Path with Heart* as a good introductory book to meditation. If you would like other recommendations, please feel free to write me at yhanda@gmail.com with your current interests and a little of your meditation background, and I'd be happy to offer my own personal recommendations suited to you.

Meditation, as I've been taught, is self-correcting. You can do a lot wrong while meditating. I certainly have, and likely will continue to do so. But by its nature, there's awareness being brought to the act—unless you're falling asleep or zoning out every single time, which is highly unlikely. And even if you're zoned out for 95% of it, there's still that 5% when you're presently awake. Even with 5% awakeness, it's eventually going to become obvious to you when something is off.

So for the first 14 to 15 years, I meditated a lot—that is, when I did meditate. I would sit for one to two hours a day. Sometimes, it felt as if I was forcing it in there. Then, a couple of months into it, I'd simply stop, out of the blue. No real reason. Just one day my willingness to meditate wasn't there. I'd think to myself, "I know meditation is amazing and wonderful. Why can't I do it every day and keep it up?" I'd sometimes beat myself up for it, and then, a couple of months would pass, and maybe I would attend a workshop, read a book, or nothing would happen at all, and I would find myself meditating again.

Stop, start, stop, start. That was my relationship to meditation. We essentially broke up a lot.

Then, a little over 15 years ago I became a daily practitioner. I can't say for sure what it was. Maybe it was just time, and that some people like me require a 10 to 15 year period of unsteady practice for it to sink in. Maybe it was karma. What I *do* know is that I made one conscious decision at that point when it all started that I hadn't made before.

I put a time limit or cap on my practice.

While I was able to sit continuously, in some semblance of meditation, for a couple hours by that time, I made a decision to *force* myself to stop at 30 minutes. It was a pivotal (or what I now believe to be pivotal) decision in my relationship to meditation, and I'm convinced that that was one of the main factors that led to my practice sustaining itself from that point forward.

I mentioned this idea earlier. Even though I didn't have the philosophical framework of *kaizen* in mind, by having a cap of 30 minutes (which for me seemed very meager at the time), I was holding myself to long-term, incremental growth in terms of the time I meditated.

One thing I soon realized was that a large part of my motivation for meditating was somehow "getting there." I couldn't have articulated where that place was, had anyone asked me, but it had something to do with "getting to" a place of peace, contentment or happiness that was more stable than what I had known before. And I had it in me, somewhere half-conscious and half-unconscious, that if I meditated more and more, I could get there and stay there, permanently!

From the outside, it may have looked like I was pursuing a simple life where I studied, exercised, ate, and meditated. But there was a huge personal agenda going on, masquerading as "spiritual work." Meditation for me wasn't just to be or to sit or anything like that. It was to get somewhere, which is to say, it was to deny where I was, or to deny my current reality. And yet, most forms of meditation are about accepting and *embracing* one's current reality. And as I would later find out, fighting reality is tremendously tiring.

So by capping my efforts at 30 minutes, I inhibited this agenda of mine, which when one thinks about it clearly, is not in alignment with most forms of meditation. But just as importantly, in regards to the 30-minute cap, I was doing myself a great favor without realizing it.

Whenever I meditated for two or three hours in one day, I unintentionally set myself up with a subtle expectation that I could do it again the next day. In fact, if I didn't do it the next day, I felt let down and disappointed. And so out of sheer willpower, I would do it anyway. Maybe for even a full week or two. But inevitably, meditation isn't synonymous with sheer willpower. This became clear to me when I began putting a time cap on my practice.

Today I see meditation as more about relaxing the mind and settling into an open awareness. Back then, it was all about getting somewhere by sheer force of will. The problem with willpower is that it runs out very quickly. It's also no fun. No wonder I would eventually quit. Completely. For weeks, sometimes months at a time.

For me, a 30-minute cap seemed very short, like I wasn't even trying. But it was perfect. I'd sit for 30 minutes, and even if I wanted to stay sitting and go "deeper," I'd get up, telling myself, "We're doing this for the long run. I don't have to get anywhere right now. I'll get to sit again like this tomorrow."

The real value in this for me was that there was very little stress in sitting the next day because in my mind it was *just* 30 minutes. Had I been thinking of sitting for three hours, my attitude would have been considerably more stressed and resistant. Instead, 30 minutes was like touching the floss box. As far as I was concerned, it was grazing a practice on my way to grabbing a shirt from the closet (since I was sitting in my walk-in closet at the time).

In this manner, I kept my practice at 30 minutes for a couple of years, and only after the "daily" part of my practice felt stable did I move it to 45 minutes, then to an hour. Now, I do something closer to 90 to 120 minutes a day. Sometimes more and sometimes less. Tracking the time doesn't seem as important to me as it once did since it's just a habit, a part of who I am, and something I love.

A few years ago, I tried committing to four hours a day, just to see if I could average that across a year. It felt a bit much. I logged everything I did. I took a partial leave from work so that I had more time for practice. In the end, I did average a little over four hours a day for the year. I also realized that I didn't get any more observable benefit from that than doing two hours a day. And with my extra time off of work, I just thought more about sex, but that's another story altogether!

Chapter 3: Why do we care about posture?

I'd like to talk a little bit about posture, starting with a little exercise. It's something I've tried out with different groups I've led or taught. I hope you'll try it with an experimental attitude and open mind.

Exercise:

Wherever you happen to be sitting right now, try sitting up straight in a relaxed way, not in a militaristic-style that's stiff and rigid with your shoulders pulled back baring your chest; instead, just relaxed and upright. Your gaze can be soft and in a slightly downcast direction. We'll call this posture #1. (See figure 1.)

Once you have a sense of posture #1, which may take just a few seconds to settle into, try "collapsing" your posture, so that your back curves, your shoulders hunch forward, your chest caves in, and your head is slightly down. (See figure 2.) We'll call this posture #2.

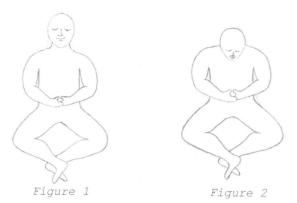

Figure 1   Figure 2

Now, try sitting back upright, but unlike posture #1, be effortful (as opposed to relaxed) in your upright quality. Stick your chest out, pull your shoulders back, look straight ahead, and hold all of that as firmly as you can. (See figure 3.) We'll call this posture #3.

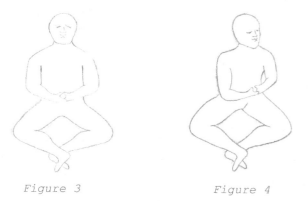

Figure 3   Figure 4

Lastly, try twisting your torso in one direction or the other. Still look in the same general direction that you were previously, but twist your torso. (See figure 4.) We'll call this posture #4.

It will be helpful for you to try the following experiment so that you can experience first-hand how your mental and emotional states are changed by how you hold your body.

There are three parts to this experiment:

Part 1: Alternate between posture #1 and posture #2.

Take the relaxed, upright posture of posture #1. As you settle into this, take note of the quality of your thoughts. By quality, I mean not just what you are actually thinking, but the tone of your thoughts. Are they expansive or contractive? Are they focused or wandering? Are they forward-looking, backward-looking, or more presently focused? And so on and so forth.

Also, take note of the tone of your emotions. Do they feel expansive or contractive? That is, are they open or closed? Are they positive, negative, or neutral? Are they uplifting, depressed, or more indifferent?

Lastly, take note of your energetic or somatic experience. Besides some of the descriptors already offered, pay attention also to how your energy changes as you move from one posture to another. Part of your energetic experience is your breath, so pay attention also to how your breath changes. Another part of your energetic experience is what you feel in your body, so pay attention to how things feel in your body.

As you hold posture #1, take note of these things, whatever comes to mind. Try not to be worried about covering everything I mentioned. Try instead to notice what comes to the forefront of your awareness. When you've noted two or three aspects of your experience of being in posture #1, slowly shift into posture #2. And as you hold posture #2, go through your experience noting two or three things that feel different to you in this posture. When you've made note of two or three things, gradually shift back into posture #1.

Go back-and-forth between the two postures about three or four times, where each time, you make note of what changes, what's different in your mental, emotional, and energetic experience between the two postures.

Try to spend about two to three minutes total.

Part 2: Do the same thing as in Part 1, but move between posture #1 and posture #3.

Part 3: Do the same thing as in Part 1, but move between posture #1 and posture #4.

End of exercise.

Although this may not exactly match your own experience, here is a summary of what most people who have engaged in this exercise with me have reported.

Posture #1: relaxed, upright.
- The breath flows easily.
- The body feels most open and relaxed.
- The mind feels more present.
- There's a greater sense of openness in contrast to any of the other postures.

Posture #2: collapsed.
- Harder to breathe (though someone once said that it was easiest to breathe this way. Later, we discovered that when sitting upright, he felt too exposed as his natural posture was very collapsed; he also confessed that he was chronically depressed).
- A feeling of laziness or loss of energy.
- Feeling depressed.
- A darker mood.
- Energy doesn't flow as well as in posture #1.
- Thoughts turn to the past more easily.

Posture #3: stiff, upright.

- A sense of needing to do things right; almost a feeling of perfectionism.
- A feeling of being stuck in that position.
- A feeling of trying to make a good impression, that is, being outwardly focused.
- Harder to breathe.
- Energy doesn't flow as well as posture #1.

Posture #4: twisted
- A feeling of forgetfulness.
- Breath is constricted.
- Thinking feels off somehow, but also, different.
- Energy doesn't flow as well as posture #1.

For most of us, when we're sitting or standing upright in a relaxed fashion, the energy flows more smoothly, our minds are clearer and more open, and it's easier to be present. In the collapsed posture #2, we tend to lose energy, and depressive thoughts and moods are more likely to appear. In addition, our thoughts tend to center on ourselves, again, mostly in a darker fashion. In the overly straight and stiff posture, we lose a sense of flow and openness, and while we don't become depressed, there's a touch of hyperness to our minds or hearts in that posture. Lastly, with the twisted postures, the energy is constricted and we tend to lose a sense of being present to the moment.

The purpose of the exercise was to give an experiential sense of how our postures can influence our breathing, our energetic levels, as well as the quality and tone of our thoughts and emotions.

If you're going to meditate, which is to go deeply within yourself, it will be important for you to do so with as little burden upon yourself as possible. In other words, you don't want to meditate with constricted breathing, low energy, a depressed mood, and so on. You want to meditate with as much clarity and openness of mind, with as full and deep a breath, with as much energy that is flowing within you, and so on. This is to say that posture is *immensely* important in the practice of meditation and in the endeavor of building a daily practice. Imagine the difference between trying to do something every day where you feel depressed while doing it versus where you feel open.

Posture is important in another important way as well. I want to share a personal story to make this point. I've also been a *tai-chi/qigong* practitioner for almost 30 years as well. For those of you who are not familiar, qigong is something like Chinese yoga. Or we can say that yoga is like Indian qigong. It's an oversimplification, but not that far off.

The word *qi* is usually translated as energy or life force, and the word *gong* means work. So, you can think of qigong as "energy work." It's the practice of learning to generate, refine, and harness the life force that exists within and outside of our bodies. There are many different forms of it, but after my first 12 years of learning and practicing various forms, I found one to be the most powerful and effective in terms of cultivating and refining this life force within me. It's a "static" form of qigong called *Zhan Zhuang* (literally meaning "standing like a post"), and is sometimes referred to as "standing qigong," or even "standing meditation." [4]

I've found it to be a powerful form of not just energy work, but of a contemplative practice. When I'm able to cultivate and refine my qi, not only does my health feel more robust, my intuition is sharper and more refined. I have even had many unexplainable, paranormal experiences that I attribute to the practice of qigong. [5]

For the past 14 years or so, standing qigong has been my primary qigong practice. I do it almost daily, and it takes me about 30 minutes to complete. For about the first three to four years when I was learning standing qigong, I practiced it two to three times a

---

[4] See Ken Cohen's excellent book, *The Way of Qigong: The Art and Science of Chinese Energy Healing* for a thorough introduction to the topic. In the end, it will be best to find a qualified teacher to experience first-hand the benefits from qigong practice.

[5] Since this is not a book on qigong, I will not go into more detail than this about the practice.

day. [At the time of this story, that's what I was doing.] I was a doctoral student and short on
time. Trying to carve out two or three 30-minute sessions in a day, when most of my day was spent in
class as a student, teaching a class, or doing research,
was a tremendous challenge. I also had other obliga-
tions, including my marriage (at the time) as well as
my 30-minute meditation practice! In addition, I
needed down time, which for me was watching an
occasional movie on DVD.

You're usually instructed to do qigong outside, in nature or in a peaceful setting, but sometimes, I wanted
(needed!) to watch a movie. So I did both together. It wasn't ideal, but I figured it was better
than not doing qigong at all.

This one time, I happened to be watching the movie
Identity, with John Cusack. It's a thriller with a
touch of horror in it. I was doing my qigong and
right at the 30-minute mark of my practice, the
movie reached its climax, a horrifically dark and
twisted ending. Or it felt immensely dark to me at
the time. So, I'm doing qigong, in a dark room,
scared out of my mind and completely freaked out
when I was supposed to be feeling peaceful and calm
from the practice. Had I been sitting there watching
the movie without qigong, I'm certain my reaction
would have been very different. I might have
thought, "Wow, what a freaky movie! What an
amazing yet unexpected ending!" And that would
have been that. But doing qigong *and* watching,

something about the darkness and twistedness of the ending went much deeper into my psyche. I felt it go deep, and in fact, the feeling of being genuinely creeped out at the thought of the scene in question stayed with me for years!

What did I learn from this? That while I'm doing qigong or meditating, I need to be careful what I expose my mind to during, and/or immediately afterwards. *The point of the story is that when we meditate, we open our minds and hearts in subtle ways.* So if you incline forward throughout your meditation session, you're basically opening the deeper parts of your psyche to depressed thoughts and moods. Put differently, if you meditate while collapsed forward and downward, you're going to create a disposition towards depression, self-doubt and discouragement. This is how it has been taught to me by a Tibetan lama.

It's one thing to normally live life with poor posture, which in itself can take away from your quality of life. But to carry that same posture into your meditation practice can exacerbate any tendencies toward mental and emotional imbalance. Remember, when we meditate, we're going deeper into our psyche. We're opening it up. We don't want to bring unnecessary negative or onerous energy into that part of our mind.

If you meditate while leaning forward, you can create a tendency toward depression. If you meditate while sitting overly straight and rigid (posture #3), you can cause a propensity toward hypertension (and I would add, perfectionism). If you meditate in a twisted posture, energy channels aren't aligned and it can lead to paranoia and warped thinking; you'll begin to think that it's a normal way of thinking even when it's not.

Again, you can go back and do the exercises and see what kinds of mental and emotional states arise when you take these various postures. By maintaining them in your meditation, across days, weeks, months, and years, you can imagine how your supposedly calming and pacifying meditation practice would lead to a cultivation instead of these undesired mental and emotional states!

In meditation it's important to have an open, natural energy flow, which is why posture is the first thing that's usually addressed in most traditions. You don't want to start meditating in the wrong way insofar as posture is concerned, or you'll build a practice on a poor foundation. That can lead to creating an inhospitable psyche. You think you're doing something good, but you may be doing more harm than good if the body isn't upright and relaxed.

Sometimes I wonder if the reason some of us don't stay with our practice is due, not to laziness or lack of dedication, but instead, to our practice stopping us for our own good. Remember that meditation has a self-correcting mechanism to it, a kind of built-in wisdom, if you will. Imagine that you're doing meditation with poor posture. It's possible something within your psyche knows this, and the intrinsic wisdom in you—within the practice itself—may be causing you to quit! It might know that if you continue with poor posture, you'll be furthering yourself from any sense of happiness, relaxation, calm, and fulfillment. On the other hand, what if we focused on maintaining an upright, relaxed posture? Maybe this becomes the key to allowing the practice to continue onward?

For some of us, checking our posture, even seeing someone who specializes in it, such as a rolfer or someone who teaches the Alexander technique, might be just the thing to get our practice back on track.

Seven-point posture

At this point, I think it's worth going over the basics of posture, sometimes referred to as the "seven point posture." This is the kind of thing you can read in just about any meditation book, or if you get basic meditation instruction at any kind of meditation center, this is what they'll teach you. What I want to do is explain, as explicitly as I'm able, why each of the following seven points of posture is important. Sometimes when we understand the reason for something, we're more inclined to do it.

1. The **back** is upright and in a relaxed fashion. Since I've already gone over this one in some depth, I won't say anything more about it.

2. With the **feet** or **legs**, the key point is to feel grounded. If sitting on the floor, one way to do that is to make sure your knees are touching the ground (see figure 5 below).

Figure 5

If you aren't flexible enough, you can use small cushions or pillows to connect your knees to the ground (see figure 6 below). The cushions "create" the ground. The idea is that by having your knees touch down, you make a wider base, or a tripod effect to help ground your energy.

Figure 6

If sitting in a chair, the feet should be *flat* on the ground. Again, the intent is to be grounded. Experiment with this the next time you're at a meeting or gathering of some kind. Try paying attention to people's legs, and particularly, their feet. Are their feet resting flat on the ground, or, like many people, is one leg resting on another in some way so that they are only "half grounded?" Some like to curl their feet up, closer to their body so that they're on their tiptoes. Others rest one leg on another while keeping the other leg stretched out so that only a heel is touching. You can see that each situation has a different level of grounding.

I find that the quality of what people speak, in terms of the groundedness of their input/comments, correlates fairly well with what their feet are doing. It's the same for me. If I'm going to contribute something in a meeting, I make sure to sit with my feet firmly planted. It grounds my energy, and thus, my attitude and my thinking.

[I don't think high heels are ideal for meditation or for coming across as being grounded in this regard.]

If you really want to ground yourself, imagine roots growing from the bottom of your feet—starting at the point of indentation in

the soles about a third of the way down from
your toes (see figure 7)—down into the
ground (see figure 8). Think of it as a tube or
an actual tree-like root, and you can send it as
deeply as you want, all the way to the center
of the earth, if you like.

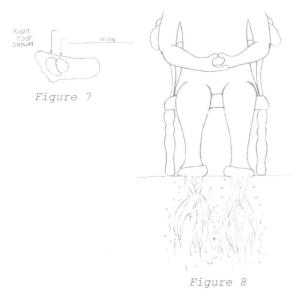

Figure 7

Figure 8

If you happen to be sitting on a cushion on
the floor, you can do the same visualization
with roots starting from your perineum downward into the earth.

At this point, your back is naturally and relax-
edly upright, and either your feet are flat on
the floor or you've formed a "tripod" with

your buttocks and both knees touching the ground or cushions.

3. With your **hands**, the easiest thing to do is to rest them, palms down, on your lap or your knees, whichever feels more comfortable to you. This is what I do.

There are meditation traditions that encourage different hand positions, called *mudras*. You might google the word "mudra" to learn more about it, if you're interested. You'll find there are a myriad of ways to configure your hands, and each is said to activate or pacify different energy systems within you.

My own tendency is not to get too technical about such things, but to listen intuitively to what feels right to me at the moment. I trust my body, and I allow it to tell me what's best in that moment, whether I need to be settled or energized, and which of my energetic subsystems might be calling for some attention. While I don't do this often, there are times when I'll play around with different mudras until I arrive at one that feels right to me. And I'll use that one. I don't care what it means or what it does. Later, if I'm curious, I might look it up, but most of the time, I don't. As I've already mentioned, usually I simply rest my hands palms down on my lap, which is the most common placement for the hands within most meditative traditions that I've come across.

There is one mudra I want to mention specifi-cally—the "cosmic mudra" or "Zen mu-dra." If you've seen pictures of Zen monks or practitioners, you will likely have seen it. In this one, your dominant hand goes un-derneath the other—both facing up—with the middle knuckle of the non-dominant hand sit-ting on top of the middle knuckle of the dom-inant one. The thumbs touch lightly. Place this just below the belly button, or if you're familiar, in front of the second chakra (see figure 9). Rest your hands on the crease in your clothing there—you needn't hold it up in the air without support or else that would eventually cause unnecessary tension.

Figure 9

I mention this mudra in particular because it's a very practical one. It can be used as a gauge or barometer of how present you are, or of your *efforts*, during meditation. You might think of effort as being one of three types. *The ideal is to have a relaxed effort,*

one that is neither too tight and overly effortful nor too loose and sloppy. You want to be
relaxed yet concentrated, easeful yet present. Not too tight, not too loose, as they say.

Sometimes you get into that nice spot. But
other times, you can get overly effortful and
strained, and at the other end of the spectrum,
you can get too relaxed and spaced out (i.e.,
no concentration).

In the cosmic mudra, your thumbs can act as
an externalized feedback mechanism for the
mind. They should be *touching lightly*. What
you'll find is that if your effort is too tense
and strained, your thumbs will start pressing
against each other (see figure 10). They'll reflect your mind in this way.

Figure 10

On the other hand, if you get too loose and
spaced out, your thumbs will collapse and fall
apart (see figure 11), which is an indication to
put in a little more effort.

By using this mudra during your meditation, you can check in with your thumbs on occasion, and therefore check into the quality of your mind and your efforts at that point in time, then make any corrections if needed.

4. The **shoulders** should not slump forward, as already mentioned, but also you don't want them pulled back tightly.

    All seven points of posture that I am outlining here can be seen as a coherent whole if you view it from the perspective of energy flow.

    Pinning your shoulders back and sticking your chest out may look bold and healthy, but the actual experience of it is one of tension. It's a posture that you have to *strain* to hold, not.one that you can relax into. This tension cuts off the natural flow of energy. And while slumping your shoulders is certainly relaxing, it doesn't allow enough openness for the flow of energy either.

This visualization I learned from a teacher of Alexander Technique (AT) might help: Imagine the upper-back being *broad* and *strong.* Then, allow the shoulders to relax down to the sides. This has a tendency to naturally open up the upper torso, including the backside and not just the front, while also broadening the shoulders in a way that doesn't cause strain.

5. The standard directions for the **head** and **chin** are to tuck the chin in slightly. I prefer the way I was taught using AT, which is to *allow the muscles in the back of the neck to release.* The key word here is "release." The head is allowed then to float up as if on its own accord. From there, *the head can turn slightly forward* (where you get the same chin tucking result).

   Notice the difference though, between tucking your chin in versus the directions from AT. With the former, there is slight tension in the back of the neck and maybe even in the jaw. With the latter, the entire process is one of *allowing* and releasing.

   If your goal is to establish a daily meditation practice, think of the difference in your unconscious (or bodily) motivation between say a 15-minute period of being tense in the body, or the same period of allowing your body into a state of openness and relaxation. Can you see how a posture of tension and stress can de-motivate and/or discourage you to actually sit down to practice?

6. The **eyes** are usually *kept softly open and slightly downcast.* You don't want to glare or focus in on anything unless you are doing a particular form of meditation that involves focusing on an external object. Instead, keep your gaze soft. Think of it as relaxing your vision. Traditionally, it's taught as picking a point that is about "16 finger widths" in front of your nose. Try it and see how it works..

Another way to approach this softening of gaze is to think of expanding your peripheral vision, or simply putting your attention more on the periphery of your visual field. Then let the eyes fall where they naturally rest.

The reason for the soft gaze, again, is to avoid tension. You can try this short exercise: Pick any nearby object and focus your vision upon it for a few seconds. Next, soften your gaze so that everything is out of focus (or you can attempt to focus on a point in midair that's about 12 inches out from your nose) and hold this for a few seconds. Then go back to the object for a few seconds, and soften for a few seconds, and so on. While going back-and-forth like this, try to become aware of the amount of tension around your eyes. What you want to settle upon in your meditation is a way of looking that causes the muscles around your eyes to be the most relaxed, without your eyes being closed.

Although the following is unlikely to be feasible unless you happen to be practicing on a mountaintop or a wide-open field, you may find that picking a point far off in the distance is also relaxing to the eyes. In fact, in the practice of qigong, we're taught to pick a view as far away as possible and place our gaze upon it. Usually, qigong is done outdoors in nature so this is fine. But in meditation, most of us are in a room, and even the view out of most windows doesn't extend for more than a few yards, if that. Therefore, softening the gaze is the expedient solution.

But the next time you find yourself outdoors in the evening, you might look at the stars and notice how your eyes relax when you gaze upon something at such a distance.

As for why we keep the eyes open, you might experiment with this too. It's been my experience—and it's usually taught like this—that when the eyes are closed, it's much too easy to get lost in thoughts and distracted by daydreams. This isn't to say that having our eyes open prevents this. I'll be the first to admit that my thoughts are frequently all over the place, regardless. And yet, I'm much quicker to notice it when my eyes are open. If they're closed, I can spend half a session lost in fantasy without even the slightest recognition that I've been off on my own mental adventure for that long!

7. Lastly, we come to the **mouth** and **tongue.** The mouth should be lightly closed so you can breathe through your nose. *Lightly* place the tongue on the upper palate of your mouth, about a quarter of an inch behind the front teeth. For most people, there is a spot around that point that is slightly indented, a bit like a pocket, which I sometimes think of as my "tongue pocket," in that my tongue fits snugly into the indentation.

In qigong, it's taught that there are various energy meridians operating within the body, with the principal channel going up the back, starting near the perineum, all the way to the top of the head. From there, it drops down the front and back to the perineum, thus creating a cycle or orbit. And yet, there is a disjunction or disconnect in the circular channel, from the "tongue pocket" to the tongue. Only when our tongue is touching the spot behind our front teeth do we complete the channel. Some teachers in the qigong tradition say that when this part of the orbit is disconnected, the energy has a tendency to stay in the head.

It's been my experience that when I'm feeling heady (as in too much energy in the head region), I can simply connect my tongue to the "tongue pocket" and imagine the energy coming down. Before I knew about this disconnect, I was never successfully able to bring the energy down. It could all be in the head. Who knows? (ha ha.)

I mentioned earlier the idea of using the thumbs on the cosmic mudra as a barometer of your mindfulness, or effort. The same can be done with the tongue. The advantage with the tongue is that you can be in a public place and still do it without looking like you're practicing or being a poser.

As with the thumbs, your tongue should be *lightly* touching. When you're over-exerting, your tongue will likely press hard against the palate. When your mind is wandering, your tongue may similarly be wandering, no longer placed on the palate, but darting around, feeling out the bottom of the mouth, or even cleaning off the backs of the teeth.

In summary, these seven points of posture are a good reminder for *easing* into meditation. Each point can be thought of as an invitation toward entering a relaxed, yet wakeful state.

In the next section, I will briefly explain a basic form of meditation, then offer an initial suggestion for starting your practice.

Chapter 4: Our minds

What do we do with our minds now that our bodies are in a relaxed and upright posture?

Although we can do a number of things, for now, I'd like to offer two possibilities. The first is a form of meditation called *shamatha* (or it's basically what goes for "mindfulness" in the West). So if you're already familiar, you may want to skip ahead to the next one.

Shamatha is usually translated as "calm-abiding" or "pacifying" meditation, and as its name implies, its purpose is to calm and steady the mind. We begin by choosing an object to *settle* the mind upon, the most common being the breath. It's possible to use things such as candlelight, a picture, the sound of a brook, and so on. The useful thing about the breath is that it always accompanies us. You could get very attached to resting the mind upon your favorite candlelight, and then, one day, it wears out, or the store runs out of it, causing panic.

The breath works nicely also because it acts as a conduit, moving us closer to our bodies. Since it's the body that breathes, as we become more attuned to our breath, we naturally become more attuned to our bodies. There are a myriad of benefits to being in touch with our bodies, including learning to listen more carefully to its intrinsic wisdom, as well as becoming more sensitized to the energy (or *qi)* that flows *through* our bodies.

So we take our posture for meditation and begin by noticing the breath. There are two common ways we can begin to settle our minds upon our breath. The first is simply to count our breaths, either in-breath or out-breath. Although I don't believe it's a matter of right or wrong which you choose, here is one heuristic for choosing. If your mind is *outwardly* focused, that is, thinking of various people to talk to, tasks you need to attend to, and other such "worldly" matters, count your in-breath, so as to bring more of your attention toward it. By bringing your attention to your in-breath, your mind can begin to collect itself *inwardly*.

On the other hand, if your mind is more *inwardly* focused, that is, very sensitive to your inner landscape, as in emotions, thoughts, and physical sensations, then count your out-breath, so as to bring more of your attention to it. By bringing your attention more to your out-breath, your mind can open up and relax. Ultimately, it's a matter of striking a balance. Choose to focus on the segment of the breath that is contrary to the state of your mind at the time that you enter your practice.

As you breathe, mentally count "one." Then, on the next breath, "two," and so on. When or if you reach "ten," start over at "one" again on the following breath. If during this time, your mind wanders off and you lose track of where you are, or you realize that your mind has somehow been counting a number but without any recollection of how you got to "eight" or even "nineteen" (yes, this can happen), just begin again at "one."

There is no goal of being a perfect counter or of bragging to your friends that you counted from one to ten many times. It's pointless to get caught up in being "successful" at this. The point is you're trying to create an anchor for your mind, which by its nature, wants to wander off. Each time it does, *gently* bring it back to your breath. And that's it. That's the entire practice.

Simple, and yet not so easy. The mind may rebel and wander restlessly. That's okay. Whenever you notice the mind wandering, simply bring your attention back to counting from "one." If it gets boring, just note that it's boring, and count from "one" onward. If the personality (ego) is insulted by this, that's fine too. Simply bring your attention back to the in- or out-breath and count from "one."

Some of you may not get bored and instead attack this with an over-zealous energy. You'll success-fully go from one to ten, over and over again. If this is the case, check your thumbs or your tongue. If they're pressing hard against one another or against the palate, this could be an indication that you're ef-forting too hard. You aren't being relaxed enough in your approach. If you then try to relax your efforts, you may slip up a bit and get sloppy. If so, you can correct back to being a little more concentrated or disciplined. Back-and-forth. The idea, again, isn't to get good at counting. It's to be present where you are, in a relaxed and alert manner. That's what get-ting good at this looks like. And as soon as you think you're good at it, you're likely lost in thought and not counting.

If you manage to stay like this for just a few minutes, your mind eventually begins to settle down. It be-gins abiding calmly. And you've been meditating!

A second way of using your breath as an object of meditation is probably better for those of you who tend to be inwardly-focused as a matter of habit. So in this case, you'll bring your focus to the out-breath. As you breathe out, imagine resting your mind on the out-breath, and filling up the room or space around you. That is, your mind (or you can think of it as your consciousness) "rides" your breath out as long as it will go. Then, when that out-breath has expired, simply *allow* the in-breath to hap-pen. Don't consciously or pro-actively breathe in. The conscious, pro-active element with this method is in the out-breath only. So, "go out" with your breath as far out as you can without strain, then *allow* for the in-breath to happen. This is all you do. If your mind wanders, simply come back to this.

If you feel uneasy that you're going "out" without ever coming in, you can visualize yourself coming back to yourself during the in-breath, but you're not trying to control the breath itself or make it be any deeper than it naturally wants to be. [If you study Eastern forms of breathing, most tend to emphasize the out-breath over the in-breath, in terms of making a complete out-breath as opposed to taking a deep in-breath.]

Further, there is no need to make any attempt to control the length of either the in- or out-breath. In both methods, you're breathing naturally.

Exercise:

Here is a short exercise to try. Take a relaxed, up-right posture, as previously discussed, choose one of the two breathing methods just described, and attempt it for three minutes.

Regardless of which method you choose, your mind will slowly begin to settle after a few minutes. Once it does, begin to be aware of the sensations in your body. It can be delightful, even pleasurable, to feel

breathing happening in your body. Perhaps you notice that?

Chapter 5: Time and location

In putting together a regular formal practice, two important details to consider are time and location.

For most people, the best times to practice formally are in the morning before the day starts or at the end of the day before bed. Having had a daily practice at both times, I can speak to the advantages of both. At one point I also had a regular afternoon practice, and I'll speak to that as well.

Morning: This is my preferred time, and where it's been for the past 13 years or so. Although I also frequently practice in the evening and sometimes in the afternoon, it's my morning practice that's the constant.

Entering a state of calm or settling down is challenging when one has to switch over from the midday hustle-and-bustle. It's a bit like trying to stand still in turbulent waters. So, first thing in the morning and end of the evening makes sense in this regard. Things are quieter, not just in terms of physical activity, but also in terms of mental chatter. But mostly, it's that our energy is least agitated at those times for most of us (with the exception of the mid-afternoon nap period, but that's also not an ideal time to meditate since one would likely just fall asleep on the cushion).

I find that starting the day off in meditation sets a good tone for the day, and I'm not a morning person by any means. I find it to be a gentle way of transitioning from sleep into wakefulness. It also gets it "out of the way," so to speak. For me, my meditation practice is possibly the most important thing I do in the day. So, I want to get to it first. I don't want to put it off. I don't want to place less important things before it. In fact, after practice comes writing for me, in terms of priorities. So, that's the order in which I conduct my day. (I should note that I usually eat a nut bar or piece of fruit to keep me going until my first meal of the day, which comes after the writing.)

Everything else that follows in the day is easy since they're lower in priority for me. In fact, during the afternoons, I'm usually scrambling about trying to create income for myself. But it's not particularly stressful (because I've already gotten the two most important things out of the way).

Evenings: When I began meditating at the age of 18, this is when I practiced, and when I finally started sitting daily, it was in the evenings as well.

One of the great benefits of practicing before bed was that it conditioned me to fall asleep quickly. I'd enter such a calm and restful state that when I was done, I'd just put my head to the pillow and fall asleep in seconds. Even though I haven't consistently meditated before bed in years, the habit of falling asleep quickly has stayed with me.

Being that I take showers and "clean off" my body in the evening, I liked the idea of "cleaning out" my mind and heart before bed through meditation as well. After a full and messy day, I always knew that I could cleanse off my mind in the evenings. There was something reaffirming for me in that, as if the practice allowed me to live my days more fully, or more messily. The reason I switched to the mornings as my "committed" sessions had to do with the fact that I found myself exhausted for some of my evening sessions. And the idea of attending to something that was so important to me, with barely any energy, no longer felt aligned with my priorities.

Mid-day: This has always been the most challenging time for me. Once I get going with my day, whether it be a workday filled with activity, social engagement, and overall busyness, or a weekend day with downtime, friends, shopping, gardening, and what have you, stopping the flow of activity by plopping myself down on a cushion and becoming quiet isn't easy. I'm reminded of the phrase, "stemming the tide."

When I was an elementary student in Japan, there was a summer tradition that involved all of the students jumping into the school pool and lining the edges about two to three wide. Upon command, we'd all swim, paddle, and walk in the same counterclockwise direction around the pool. After a while, we had created a flow so it felt effortless to keep moving forward, in the same direction. Then, when the teacher blew his or her whistle, we were supposed to switch and go in the opposite (or clockwise) direction around the pool. This was the fun part! Despite our valiant efforts at swimming and walking against the current, most of us would find ourselves drifting backwards! I loved this part the most. It was like being in a dream, where I'm trying to go one way, and every part of my body is trying, and yet I keep moving backwards!

This is what practicing in the afternoon can feel like for the first few minutes, because for most of us, a certain flow of activity has been established in our being. Trying to sit *formally* in the midst of that flow isn't easy. For this reason, I don't recommend trying to set up a daily practice in the middle of the day for starters. There *are* other *informal* practices one can learn later that work well in the midst of all activity, but for now, the focus of this book is on building a daily *formal* practice. And for that, I believe the beginning and end of the day are ideal times.

Now let's discuss location. If you use the same place for meditation each day, there will be a mental and emotional association of that place, with entering a state of calm or presence. You could also think of it as imbuing a specific location in your home with a particular meditative energy to support your practice.

For years, I made do with what I had, which was mostly walk-in closets. I simply put a cushion at the back, closed the door (or left it slightly ajar), and sat. Personally, I found this satisfactory. It created quiet and a sense of space for me. When I lived with a partner, I simply put a sign up on the door that said, "Meditating. Please do not enter," and since I was consistent in the times I meditated, she was easily able to accommodate me.

I've also practiced in unused portions of bedrooms that were passageways to getting somewhere else in the room. I didn't feel as settled in such places and would have preferred a corner of the room. But in these situations, it wasn't a feasible option.

If you have the inclination, you can create an altar-like space. I generally put a low table in front of me (since I sit on the ground), with a candle and images of people or objects that I find inspiring in some way. Be careful with the candle though. When I first started, my "altar" was my word processor (I had a low-tech computer whose sole function was word processing), and I lit a candle on top of it. One time, I dozed off during meditation and woke to find a hole burned through the top of the word processor, as the candle had melted the plastic through to the electronics!

It's important to create a regular location or space for your practice that creates a desire to go deeper into meditation. Or you could think of it as somehow evoking a quality of the sacred and divine.

For the past seven years or so, I've had a room devoted entirely to my meditation practice. It's an enormous luxury. I sometimes go into the room just to settle, even if I don't want to meditate. For me, the room is imbued with a sense of openness and tranquility. I don't do things like eat a meal or have sex in there. Or watch Netflix on my laptop.

I'm blessed to have such a space, and yet, it's been a long time coming, and I don't consider it a necessity. Even the open energy I spoke of, I recognize, is in me as result of my practice. I could move to a new location and build that same quality. And if someone else were to move into my current home, but failed to practice, I know that the quality of peace (tangible enough that most people who visit my home can feel it), would fade in time.

So try not to get wrapped up in a kind of "spiritual materialism" that leads you to believe that you need to remodel your home and build a meditation room. It's good to be modest in the beginning. The corner of a bedroom or living room is sufficient, in my experience. There can even be a spirit of humility in that, which in itself can support your burgeoning practice.

If you're in a corner of a room and want a shrine of sorts, buy one of those wooden platforms that attach to the corner wall, place a few trinkets on it that you find precious or inspiring (maybe an image of something that's sacred or heart-opening for you), and call that your shrine. You could even post a semi-circular curtain to enclose the space.

The higher priority must be in recognizing that constancy of location supports constancy of practice. Anything more can become a distraction and even take away from your practice. Consider that the meditators of old sat in caves where they didn't have designer cushions, aromatherapy candles, intricate statues and statuettes, nor even the comforts of thermostat-controlled temperature.

—Week one

One of main purposes of this book is to try to lay out a plan for you so that by the time you finish reading it, you will have a consistent daily meditation practice.

I hope that you'll take your time through this 12-week process as outlined. You might choose to modify some portions, but the key idea is to consider long-term, incremental, and continuous growth. Some of the time suggestions may be too much or too little for some of you, so please, do make modifications as you see fit. The goal as I am setting it here, is that you will have a 21-minute daily meditation practice by the end of the 12 weeks. I've chosen 21 minutes simply because twenty minutes feels like a good and modest daily practice to me, and one more than that is a number that a vocal teacher I had the pleasure of meeting explained to me as being the right amount of time to connect inwardly.

Some of you may choose a more modest goal of 10 minutes a day, and for others, you may want to get up to an hour per day. If your goal is under 20 minutes per day, then my suggestion is to cut the times I offer in half for all the weeks to follow. If your goal is over 20 minutes per day, my suggestion is to pace yourself according to the way I've set out for the first 12 weeks, and simply keep growing your practice across the next few years, until you reach your goal.

For this first week, I encourage you to do three things:

1. Decide upon a *regular* time for meditating. As I've suggested before, fairly soon upon awakening in the morning or just before bed in the evening are ideal for most.

   When deciding, you might mentally make a note of which times feel more settled for you, as a criterion for selection. That is, choose the time that *when you think about that time for meditation, you feel more relaxed and your breath feels more open.* Trust that feeling and go with it. If it isn't the best time, change it next week. But go with what feels more settled in your body when you hold the thought that you'll be meditating during that time.

   If this seems a bit abstruse, do it this way. Take out a piece of paper and write on it, "1. First thing in morning 2. After breakfast in morning 3. Around noon 4. Afternoon 5. Early evening 6. Before bed." Put your finger on the paper starting with #1 while asking yourself, "Is this a good time?" and notice your breath. Is it open and relaxed? Or is it shallow and even stifled? Go through each until you find the option where your breath feels most relaxed and open. Choose that one. If there's no difference, just choose one that you like.

There's no point spending more than a minute trying to decide upon a time. You can always change it. So allow your body to pick a time for now (as explained in the previous paragraph), and try it out with an experimental spirit. You can pick any of the other times for the following week if the chosen one for this week doesn't work out.

2. Decide upon a place in your house. I suggest a place *in* your house and not outside, unless the weather in your area permits you to sit there every day of the year. You're aiming for regularity and consistency, and it helps to have that one place you can go to again and again. If you have more than one possible location, try sitting there and seeing how it feels. If your body feels more relaxed and your breath feels more open, then that's your spot.

Don't worry about finding the *perfect* spot. Go with "good enough." But again, make sure that your body feels relaxed when you consider it as your meditation spot.

Once you decide upon the location, you can even put together a small altar if that's to your liking. Or if not an altar, put a marking or small border, or even the placement of a chair or cushion, so your chosen spot is somehow marked off as a place of practice for you. As with the time, try to stick with this spot for the first week. If it doesn't work out, you can always switch in the second week.

3. Once you've chosen the time and place for your practice for the week, when that time arrives, take a seat or cushion and go through the seven points of posture, making sure to check your grounding. Then set an intention to be present to your breath, and take three breaths with as much presence and awareness as you can bring. If you happen to check out for two of the three breaths, no matter. You've done your best for now, and you're done!

The entire thing should take no more than a minute, from taking your seat to the end.

Try not to be a perfectionist about your three breaths. Even if you space out for all three, once you've taken the three breaths, you're done with your practice for the day.

Same goes for posture. Run through the seven points quickly. You're using this week, partly, to familiarize yourself with the seven points of posture. You might even jot down the seven points on a piece of paper, or open the book next to you so you can learn to quickly run through them when you sit.

Remember this is akin to touching the floss box. You're simply trying to coax yourself into the habit of taking your seat.

Many seasoned meditation practitioners will say that the hardest thing in meditation is "getting to the cushion." Once there, something else takes over, and it's not as hard to sit for long durations. But it's getting there that's often the block for many meditators. So for now, that's the focus. You're trying to create the habit of "getting to the cushion," but without the burden of any expectations of sitting there for a longer time.

We'll continue to build upon this in the coming weeks, but for now, you're just touching the floss box! My suggestion is to spend the next week committing to this simple practice. If you're going to read out of this book, you might read over what you've read up until this point but not forward. After you've practiced for a week in the manner prescribed, then you might consider moving onto the next two chapters.

Chapter 6: Bodhicitta

I'd like to introduce a word, *bodhicitta*. It's made up of two words, *bodhi* and *citta*. The words bodhi and Buddha are both etymologically derived from the same root *budh-* (meaning "to awaken, become aware, notice, know or understand"). Bodhi is usually translated as "enlightened" or "awakened," just as the word Buddha means "one who is enlightened" or "one who is awakened."

Citta is oftentimes translated as "mind." If you ask someone in the West to point to the mind, they would most often point to their head. If you ask people from some Asian cultures to point to the mind, they would point to their hearts. The Pali-English dictionary suggests citta is more the emotive side of what we call "mind" in the West. And yet, citta also involves our intentions and motivations. One could also think of it as one's "state of mind," which connotes not just the cognitive aspect of "mind" as culturally conceived in the West.

Personally, I find the translation of citta into "heart-mind" the best solution, despite its awkwardness. So bodhicitta could be thought of us "enlightened heart-mind" or "awakened heart-mind." Breaking the latter down, one could think of bodhicitta as "awakened heart" + "awakened mind." Think of these then **as two facets of this one thing** called bodhicitta.

Traditionally, in terms of how it's conceptualized, bodhicitta is said to have *two* aspects. One is called *relative* bodhicitta and the other *absolute* bodhicitta. *Relative* bodhicitta is sometimes called compassion, loving-kindness, or skillful means. This is likely the image conjured in most Western minds when hearing the phrase "awakened heart." Absolute bodhicitta is sometimes called emptiness, wisdom, or spaciousness. If you think of Buddha's mind, you might imagine it as having a quality of infinite spaciousness and wisdom, and it's likely captured by the phrase, "awakened mind."

Bodhicitta then subsumes both aspects, the warmth and tender-heartedness of compassion as well as the clarity and luminosity of spaciousness. [6]

So again, think of bodhicitta as "awakened heart" *and* "awakened mind." Both together. But what

---

[6] There are more technical and comprehensive definitions for this word. I have chosen to focus on what I feel are the relatable aspects of it.

about bodhicitta in terms of how it shows up in our lives? For now, I want to focus on relative bodhicitta, which in itself has two aspects.

Relative Bodhicitta

If you were to carefully observe and inquire into others (as well as yourself), looking beyond the facades, listening past the stories, you would likely notice that all of us, in one form or another, are seeking some form of happiness and trying to avoid suffering. What you also might see is that most of us are failing pretty miserably at this—that is, when we look beneath the surface.

Some of us may be resigned to having an occasional reprieve from suffering, and we settle for that. This isn't genuine happiness, but more a *temporary* alleviation of our unhappiness with which we content ourselves. Others of us may be happy for a moment, but then become dissatisfied or want something better. If a little is good, we want just a little more. Or we may stick our heads in the sand hoping no one notices the degree of self-doubt and inner angst brewing just beneath the surface. And still others may build walls against all the things we believe bring us unhappiness, cordoning ourselves off from living a full and expansive life, and are left still wanting. In turn, we may choose to put labels on others who threaten our fragile sense of happiness and peace.

Most of us are doing all these things, in one form or another, however obvious or subtle the form of it may be. This doesn't begin to include those whose life conditions are so harsh and unaccommodating that any sort of moderate happiness feels out of reach.

We all seem to want stable and *lasting* happiness, but there is *seemingly* little of that to be had, as things are in constant flux.

Even for the happiest among us, there is sometimes a voice in the back of the mind that says that there still might be a slightly better kind of happiness just around the corner! It could be a relationship, a more fulfilling job, more money, more robust health… Or just *more* happiness. And then if we happen to obtain the thing that's around the corner, what happens? There's a new corner!

In this constant pursuit of happiness, there's often a sense of *more* or *better*, and none of it is stable and lasting. If you watch people closely, or when we look at ourselves carefully, most of us experience this cycle of thinking that if we just get this or that, something great will happen. But it rarely does. Or it does for a very short time, and before too long, we're on to the next thing.

We can meet the love of our lives, and maybe we're happy for a few months or years, but then at some point it becomes work, and as a reaction, some part of us sets up a new agenda. Maybe if we had a better job, a bigger house, or children? Or more depth to the relationship? There's a continual mapping of possible happiness or salvation into the future, sometimes subtle, sometimes not.

When we see this state of affairs very clearly, whether in ourselves or others, one possible reaction is lovingkindness and compassion. When we genuinely see this perpetual cycle of seeking, finding, disappointment, and back to seeking—that is, when we see someone sincerely seeking happiness, and they don't find it to be stable or lasting in any meaningful way—a sense of compassion or care can be a natural response. This natural compassion is one aspect of relative bodhicitta.

From there, maybe we try helping others whom we see struggling. When we do this, we can feel good, but that good feeling doesn't last either. Maybe we feel good for an hour. A day. Maybe we become addicted to helping people, so that we can feel good more frequently. There are people who are really good helpers, and they're wonderful people. But many get burned out in one way or another, some to the point of resentment, and others I know stuff their feelings with food. Many also stop taking care of themselves. And so on.

I speak partly from personal experience. I know for myself, that I try to help others and I feel good about it for a while. I also don't want to turn helping people into an addiction, so I examine myself and ask, what's going on with me? What I recognize is that while I can be happy and grateful while attempting to help others, if that's all I concern myself with—that is, my own feelings in the endeavor—I'm missing the point. Helping others isn't about feeling better about myself, although it can be a motivating factor. Ultimately, I want to take into consideration my effect upon the other, for that can be a motivating factor for my own inner growth. If I seem to fall short of what I think possible in my capacity for helping another, that can become an incentive to attending to deeper inner growth. And this process begins with attending more to the other's *actual* welfare rather than to my own happy feelings within the act of helping.

I'm reminded of educational studies that analyze where teachers focus their attention in the classroom. In brief, beginning teachers tend to be focused on *their own* actions. After teaching a class, such teachers tend to give narratives centered around whether they, as the teacher, took helpful or unhelpful actions during class. For example, "I thought the lecture was clear" or "I could've answered the student's question better." Yet, after a few years of teaching, these same teachers shift their focus to their students. More experienced teachers' narratives tend to be centered around their students' actions and thinking, such as "Johnny's response to my question was very insightful for the other students" or "I was surprised that the students were able to generate five different solutions to the problem."

Similarly, I think it's natural in the beginning to focus on how it feels for us when helping others. In time, this focus naturally shifts to how others are being affected by our efforts. At first, that focus may be on the immediate feelings of the other, and after a while, it can shift more to the long-term welfare of the other.

In this regard, I think about the help and support I've attempted to offer others and wonder if I've ever really helped anyone to truly transform their state of mind so that they're deeply settled in lasting happiness. I'm not sure I have. You can look at people like Jesus, Buddha, Gandhi, Mother Teresa, Martin Luther King Jr; they've transformed themselves and many others. When I consider what might be the difference between them and me, the one primary difference that I can discern is capacity. Our potential is the same, or I'd like to believe it is—and yet, our current capacity is different. We're all humans, but they seem to possess greater capacity.

I want to be honest with myself about this. I know I'm limited so I want to increase my capacity, but that's just another way of saying that I seek enlightenment, or a stable and profound happiness. Unless I've found a stable form of happiness, my capacity to help others to find such happiness is limited. In the 12-step programs, there's a saying, "You can't give away what you don't have." Basically this means that if I haven't struggled through my own ignorance around some issue, and I'm still ignorant, then I'm not in a position to help someone else to become less ignorant in that area. *I* have to become less deluded myself. In other words, if I want to affect transformation in others, I have to affect transformation in myself.

As I've mentioned, relative bodhicitta has two aspects. One is the natural compassion toward all beings in seeing the nature of suffering and how it permeates all of our lives. The other is a desire or commitment to transform oneself so as to increase one's capacity to *actually* benefit others in a genuinely meaningful manner. The latter is usually phrased as an intention to gain complete enlightenment, but enlightenment is simply stable happiness, or the most profound form of happiness. One could even think of it—recalling the meaning of bodhi—as an intention to becoming awakened. This two-fold intent of compassion and commitment toward awakening is relative bodhicitta. It's not just one or the other. It's both.

If all we're doing is being compassionate and trying to help others without any real practice or movement toward self-transformation, there's a good chance our compassion will wilt into sentimentality, projection, and helplessness or overwhelm. We likely won't be helping beyond the surface appearance of things, or even if we are, we'll stay limited in our capacity to help, while inevitably suffering from burnout in one form or another.

Another common thing I've seen is that such people—myself included at times—stop taking care of ourselves. That's a good time to pause, "Maybe I'm being too focused on the helping-others side of things?" We've lost balance and lost sight of working on ourselves. In fact, *practicing and moving toward self-transformation can be one of the most profound forms of self-care or self-love,* in addition to its benefit toward others.

On the other hand, if the urge for practice and self-transformation is being attended to without compassion or care for others, there's usually something missing. In short, the rest of the universe (outside of us) is missing. We don't want our thinking to be, "I'm going to meditate until I'm enlightened, and once I am, see you all later! I'm going be blissed out of my mind, and the rest of you are all on your own!"

It's taught that a practitioner can practice for hours and hours, but without bodhicitta, it has little value compared to someone who practices for a few seconds with bodhicitta. From this point of view, practicing without bodhicitta is practically worthless, as it becomes primarily a project of self (or ego)—the exact thing a practice is meant to alleviate or eradicate, since it's the ego self itself that is considered the root

cause of our suffering. So, practicing without bodhicitta doesn't lead to true liberation, and as such, bodhicitta is considered one of the most important
qualities, if not the most, to bring into our practice.

Yet, there's also a subtle payoff or consequence of
bodhicitta. In particular, the altruistic aspect of
it. Trying to do something without the rest of the
universe is a lonely and arduous task, and you aren't
likely to persist through difficult or challenging
stretches.

I'd like to illustrate this through a personal story. After graduating from high school, I went to NYU
Tisch School of the Arts because I wanted to become
a screenwriter. Once there, I switched over to writing plays because somehow it was a trendier thing to
be doing in NYC. About a year into the program, I
began focusing my energies toward writing short stories. Then I dropped out for a while, only to return to
Pasadena City College as a ceramics major. I
quickly burned out on that and switched to psychology. Looking back, I didn't care about others—I just
wanted to figure myself out while fixing others. Then I realized I couldn't fix people, but needed
to fix society instead, so I began studying sociology. Next, I decided to study music. If I'm being

generous with myself, I would say I was *searching*. If I'm not being so generous, I'd say I was a confused mess.

I flipped through majors at a clip of about one major per semester. And almost every time, I chose self-fulfillment and/or recognition. I frequently fantasized about the various acceptance speeches I would give for the awards I would win. After floundering about like this for a few years, I met someone who would later become a mentor to me. During our very first conversation, I told him what I had been up to and he told me I could continue this cycle of starting-and-quitting, and maybe even major in underwater basket-weaving if I wanted. *Then he asked me the most important question I had been asked in my life up until that point,*

When and how in your life have you helped someone else?

There was no accusatory tone to his question. It was laid out as a simple question, and yet, I was aghast, embarrassed, and ashamed. The question was posed as if a clear mirror had been laid in front of me. I immediately thought of my sister who seemed to relish helping people. I couldn't think of one incident where I had seriously considered another's welfare. I realized that I didn't really even like people.

Then I remembered a time I helped someone in math, not as a paid tutor, but as a friend. Since math came easy to me, and it was a struggle for a few of my friends, I occasionally tutored them for free. I hadn't thought anything of it since it seemed the natural thing to do. John, this elder mentor figure, then suggested I switch my major to math, and work my way up so I could pass along knowledge to others—become a math teacher of some kind. Something in his words rang true to me. I found them comforting and yet inspiring, but mostly, I recognized there wasn't the usual sense of self-involvement, self-seeking and an agenda for recognition and appreciation. He was simply suggesting a path where I could contribute and help. So I switched over to being a math major.

In the subsequent months and years, I had many moments when I wanted to quit my schooling. Something along the order of 50 to 100 times a year. It was likely a habitual response by that point. And yet, I didn't quit. It seemed as if each time I decided that I would, forces conspired against me. People showed up out of nowhere to deter me from quitting. Or something or someone reminded me of why I started on this path to begin with.

Despite all my resistance to continuing, I somehow felt supported by the universe around me. A lot of times, I even felt a quiet joy about it. There was something about it that felt profoundly connecting for me. Something about it felt right. Before long, I completed my bachelor's and master's degrees in mathematics, and finally, my Ph.D. Eventually I became a professor of mathematics and mathematics education, as my doctorate was in mathematics education with a focus around phenomenology.

I had pursued all of the prior endeavors that I thought were my interests when they were motivated instead by some egoistic need for recognition and acknowledgement. And the one thing that lasted had very little to do with that ego or "self," but focused more on others. Granted, I liked mathematics and I was decent at it, so it wasn't like I was torturing myself in order to contribute to the world. But somehow this motivation to contribute held and sustained itself. Many of the things I pursued for self had a feeling of, "*I'm* the one doing it." But when it became more about supporting and contributing to the welfare of others, the feeling was more along the lines of the entire universe supporting me, which felt magical at times.

Though I don't have empirical evidence past my own anecdote and a few I've heard from others, I take it as a truism that *if you do things just for yourself, the effort doesn't last. On the other hand, if you do things with the thought of others, it has a greater potential for sustaining itself.* Of course, this isn't the only benefit of considering others in our endeavors. We'll generally be happier and more successful by doing so.

Which brings me back to what this book is about— building a daily meditation practice. Sometimes, we overlook the fact that the key to sustaining any endeavor is that we're not doing it entirely on our own. It's a much easier haul when we include the rest of the universe with us, strangely enough.

I occasionally glance at the website quora.com, where I follow some interesting people and read what they have to say on different issues. Sometimes I even answer questions but not often. One time there was a question asking, "How can I learn to be more persistent if I'm more interested in what could be than what is?"

I responded as follows (starting with a math joke, of course):

> *A doctor, a lawyer and a mathematician were discussing the relative merits of having a wife or a mistress.*
> *The lawyer says: "For sure a mistress is better. If you have a wife and want a divorce, it causes all sorts of legal problems."*
> *The doctor says: "It's better to have a wife because the sense of security lowers your stress and is good for your health."*
> *The mathematician says: "You're both wrong. It's best to have both so that when the wife*

thinks you're with the mistress and the mistress thinks you're with your wife—you can do some mathematics."

So, my sense is that you likely haven't found *your* "mathematics." That is, the thing you'd want to do more than a wife *and* a mistress! I can relate to and understand your tendencies since it describes my own. I've had to search for those things that I flat-out love in the deepest and most sustaining way imaginable.

Speaking of "love," here's another thing I've found useful in my own life. Many years ago someone said to me, "That which we love will sustain us while that which we have passion for will burn us up." So try to get clear on whether what you're doing is a love or a passion. I'm not trying to turn passion into a dirty word here. I'm just trying to suggest you look for that thing you love (and maybe even have passion for) that *sustains* you—in other words, something that *lasts* within your life, and not something that you burn out on.

In my life, as well as in the lives of others I know, there's one quality that's inherent in something that sustains itself—*It benefits others on some level.* Somehow, that's the magical ingredient. If your motivation for doing something is entirely about you, it won't sustain itself. It can't. It's like a black hole that caves in on itself. No other part of the universe will support you in that endeavor.

And yet, if you have even the slightest tinge of an altruistic motivation in there, and your efforts are contributing to the world around you on some level, the world responds in like. **You'll feel the support of the universe to the extent that you're intending to support the universe around you.** And it isn't hard to keep something going when a lot of the universe is regularly supporting and cheering you on in your endeavor.

But this doesn't mean going around just helping people for no reason. You want to find the convergence of what you love with your capacity to benefit others—where your desires meet with your talents. In the end, I believe that most successful and happy people in this life are people who have found that place.

When others find out about my meditation practice, they sometimes tell me that they, too, love meditation in that it helps them to feel calm and peaceful, or that it gives them a centered "feeling." And yet, they have a hard time getting back into it. They would love to meditate daily, but they don't. Some have had this relationship to meditation for a long time.

A few tell me about external factors that keep them from meditating, the most frequent being a lack of time, but deep down they know this isn't it. They know that they could easily cut out some other non-essential activity from their day to make time for meditation, and they simply don't.

When people tell me these things, I sometimes ask, "Why do you meditate?" Or, "Why do you like meditating?"

Here's a list of the most common responses to that question (something you've read in this book already):

- My life is so much better when I meditate regularly.
- I feel so wonderful and centered when I meditate!
- I enjoy the calm and peace of meditation, and it would be wonderful to have that as a daily part of my life.
- I need it!
- It helps me to overcome my anger.
- I like or believe in the philosophy of Buddhism, and I read in a book that it's important to meditate regularly.

Note how each of these reasons, while perfectly reasonable in and of themselves, lack any focus on others. In other words, they're based on self—entirely upon self—at least as consciously voiced. Granted, it's a subtle form of self, but it's still self. All this is to say, the motivations lack the twofold intention of bodhicitta. They address the growth component, but not the benefiting-of-others component. In short, *the endeavor of meditation has been turned into a self-seeking activity.*

It's not a surprise to me then that their relationships to meditation are tenuous. When one's practice fails to include some semblance of "bodhicitta," (which I use here as shorthand for growth orientation + focus on benefiting others)—that is, when it fails to include some movement toward awakening for the purpose of benefiting others—it loses the support of the universe.

If I want to create something sustainable in my life, I infuse the intention of bodhicitta into that endeavor. Put in pragmatic terms, I want this pursuit to have (1) growth for myself and (2) value for others.

I can examine my own life and look at different parts of it (i.e., career, hobbies, relationships, etc.), and I can see how much or how little of this growth for myself and value for others is involved in each of these aspects and pursuits, and there's a direct relationship to how happy I am, how much peace I experience, and how successful I am in that area. When there's very little of these two qualities, or just one and not the other, I find that I experience less peace and meaning in such areas.

When I met the person who would become my wife, I entered the relationship with the motivation of growth. And as I grew up in that relationship, I learned to care for her welfare. I didn't enter the relationship for sex, good times, or the motivations I would act upon later in my life, to little avail. When we ended our relationship as a couple, we remained very close. I would even consider her one of my closest friends. There's something lasting about the relationship, despite the change in form.

If you want to persist at meditation, it helps to have a practice that bears fruit, which from the perspective of Dharma is having a mind-stream less burdened with clinging, anger, and ignorance, as opposed to a temporary "feel good" situation that disappears as soon as you get up from the cushion, or fades over the subsequent minutes or hours. And yet, meditating solely for one's own peace is just that, a temporary "feel good" endeavor, as the degree to which a pursuit is run solely by the agenda of the self is the degree to which it will likely fail to bear the aforementioned fruit. Stated in its logically-equivalent contrapositive, if you want a practice to bear fruit, it needs to include consideration of others, and how you can bring benefit to them. Otherwise, what's the point?

Bodhicitta can support a daily meditation practice in another way. Think of the ultimate goal of meditation, as far as how it's couched in most Eastern traditions. In short, the goal is to gain complete enlightenment, which you might think of as the ultimate and most stable form of happiness, clarity, awakeness, and so on. And yet, every description that you come across on enlightenment involves the attainment of deep and profound compassion and concern for the welfare of others. It would be a complete oxymoron to consider an enlightened being who happened not to care about anyone else, or maybe just loved their family but considered everyone else as negligible. It doesn't fit with any image of enlightenment, nor does it make any sense. What would be the point of enlightenment if it turned you into a stingy jerk or an asshole?

In fact, the word bodhicitta is meant to describe the heart-mind of a Buddha, that is, an "awakened heart and mind." In other words, bodhicitta is not just a healthy intention to help support practice. It's the goal! [7]

––––––––––––––––––––––––

[7] Disclaimer: I realize that for some adherents of Zen, the statement of such a goal would seem to place an obstacle to true practice and to genuine compassion, or *unconditioned* compassion. Please note that I am talking about things at a much more ordinary level.

In light of that, imagine a practitioner who meditates without much concern for others, even holds others in utter disdain or hatred. But this person meditates fervently! Such a person may make huge strides in their capacity for insight and clear seeing, but at some point, there's going to be tremendous inner conflict for this person, because moving toward enlightenment, by definition, is moving toward an awakened mind *and heart*. They would eventually have a choice: to open up to compassion for others, or abandon the endeavor of moving toward enlightenment (or the deepest happiness). We can imagine our fictional practitioner is a serious and sincere one, so there's hope that he or she would open up to compassion and continue with his or her practice.

But imagine how much simpler it would have been had this same practitioner started with an intention of bodhicitta from the very beginning. There would not be the tense drama. It would have made for a more gradual and gentle movement toward the same goal.

Meditation is inherently self-corrective. I sometimes wonder when someone has a practice that is on-and-off, whether it's the self-corrective nature of practice that's causing the "off" portion of their practice. Maybe this person meditates mostly to feel good—to feel calm, peaceful, or centered—and little else. If one persisted without considering others, maybe it would foster a narcissistic personality or one that prided itself on its own self-satisfaction. Perhaps the practice gives way, so that the self-centered qualities don't go too deeply into the psyche.

I'm speaking from my own experience as well. When I had an on-and-off practice, I rarely considered how my practice would allow me to be more helpful to others.

So far, I hope I've persuaded you of the value of infusing your meditation practice—or any endeavor, for that matter—with an altruistic bent combined with the desire for inner growth in support of that altruistic spirit. You aren't required to use the word bodhicitta. I use it mainly because it reminds me of the two important things in this life—growing toward greater awakening and helping others—in one compact word.

You can't have one without the other. As we grow, our capacity to help others increases, and as we help others, we naturally feel motivated to continuing our growth. But also, as we see the struggle that we all share, the motivation for both increases.

I want to share a bit more about how Buddhists consider bodhicitta, in relation to karma.

I don't intend to steer too far away from the basic premise of this book, which is to help you to build a daily meditation practice. So I won't define what karma is in any rigorous way. There are excellent books for that, such as Tsong-kha-pa's *The Great Treatise on the Stages of the Path to Enlightenment (Tib. Lam rim chen mo).* For our purposes, think of karma in terms of "good karma" which leads to happiness of varying degrees, and "bad karma," which leads to varying degrees of suffering.

One metaphor for karma is to consider it as the wake of a boat moving through water. The wake you leave is your karma, both good and bad. It's said that bodhicitta has a particular effect upon karma, that it amplifies our good karma and weakens or nullifies our bad karma. If you think of it in terms of the wake, then bodhicitta allows for the bad karma to be left behind while it pulls forward our good karma to bear fruit in our current or future life (and if reincarnation is a hard sell for you, think of a future life as tomorrow or next week).

Another metaphor for how bodhicitta affects our bad karma is to imagine a repository of our bad karma at the bottom of the ocean. *Whatever sinks to the bottom will bear fruit* as part of our bad karma.

Now, imagine two people, one with bodhicitta and the other without. In a moment of carelessness, each commits a harmful act, only the person with bodhicitta commits the larger negative act. So, his bad karma is the size of a house while the bad karma of the bodhicitta-less person is the size of a fist. Certainly, the bad karma associated with the size of the house is worse. But bodhicitta can be thought to have a hollowing effect—that is, the person with the house-sized bad karma possessing bodhicitta, now has a hollow house, or basically, a shell of a house. The one without bodhicitta has bad karma the size of a fist, but since he lacks bodhicitta, it stays solid and heavy. The house floats on the surface of the water while the fist sinks to the repository at the bottom. And remember, it's this repository that bears fruit.

In this way, bodhicitta is said to have a protective function against our own negative karma. Naturally, this doesn't mean we can just attack people using the excuse that we have bodhicitta in our hearts. Certainly, if we had bodhicitta in our hearts, we wouldn't think to do that unless under the most extreme circumstances, and even then, we might find ways of avoiding it.

This notion is similar to what some Christians speak of, that if one accepts Jesus as a personal savior and lives his or her life according to "God's will" while loving others, one's "sins are washed away."

There's a fairly clean mapping between seeking enlightenment (Dharma) and living according to God's will (Christianity), and benefiting others (Dharma) and loving others (Christianity). And the result seems similar—bad karma is negated (Dharma) and one's sins are wiped clean (Christianity); good karma is pulled forward to bear fruit in the future (Dharma) and one's life is blessed (Christianity).

This has been a brief exploration of bodhicitta. There are many practices in Buddhism that help us to cultivate this quality within ourselves, one of the most prominent being the practice of *lojong*. (Again, there are excellent books on this topic including most books by Pema Chodron, but that is beyond the scope of this book.)

And yet, without the *container* of a regular practice, we will be hard-pressed to develop bodhicitta in any depth.

Chapter 7: The container of a meditation practice

I placed a jar in Tennessee,
And round it was, upon a hill.
It made the slovenly wilderness
Surround that hill...

—Wallace Stevens, "Anecdote of the Jar"

Imagine a jar as in the poem by Wallace Stevens. That jar is a container existing *in space.* As a container, its primary function is to create an inside and an outside—that is, it demarcates space in relation to itself.

When I think of a *formal* meditation practice, I also think of it as a container, but not one that exists in space *but in time.* It's a temporal container. It too marks an inside and an outside—there is what happens inside the practice, and what happens outside of it.

A high school algebra class is an example of a temporal container. A bell signals the beginning as well as the end. There is also the class that occurs in the middle. The bells demarcate time the way the walls of a jar mark off space.

Right now, if you've kept up with the first week's exercises, there's a modest container of three breaths. If you've been able to do this on a daily basis, it means you created a daily container— both of a psychic and temporal nature—where you've been able to keep out the various mundane activities of living for those three breaths.

The scholar and mythologist, Joseph Campbell has called such containers "sacred spaces." For him, a sacred space is an "absolute necessity" for having an inner life. He wrote of the importance of such sacred spaces for artists and creative people, that one of the primary commitments of the artist is to create a sacred space within which he or she can attend to his or her art on a regular, if not daily basis. The container must have walls strong enough to keep out the everyday, mundane activities for however long the commitment, whether it's a few minutes or a few hours, each day.

Similarly then for meditation, we need a container with strong walls if we want a daily practice. I've heard it said that if you were to make a list of the things you need to get done in your life, it would be never-ending. A person can stay busy until the day they die. *But if you want to meditate, at some point you simply have to make a decision to stop with the daily activities, sit down and turn inward. There's never going to come a time when all of life's tasks will be finished.* It's important to acknowledge and accept this first. If you're waiting for a time when all will be done, you'll never have the motivation needed to practice daily.

This is what a container for a practice is like. You *stop* and then say, "I'm going to practice." This is the beginning of the container. From there, if you build the walls of the container so that the everyday activities don't enter in, this is the continuation of your practice. For example, if you're practicing meditation and suddenly think, "I should check Facebook," and then you get up, grab your phone and go to Facebook, you've broken the wall of the container.

For now, if you're keeping pace with the suggested exercises, you have your container. You simply take a seat, examine your posture, and take three breaths, "one... two... three..." And you're done! That's your container. That's the start. That's touching the floss box.

From this point, it can grow and expand. Eventually, it might be 30 minutes a day. At that point, you have a daily container and for those 30 minutes, you aren't beset by various worldly pursuits and endeavors—i.e., checking emails, reading the news, chatting with friends, buying groceries, and so on. It's an amazing and invaluable gift to give to ourselves.

Also, it's been my experience that *the stronger and more extensive the daily container, the stronger and deeper the energy that can arise from within. And the greater the energy that arises, the greater the potential and capacity for transformation.*

There's a saying that God never gives us more than we can handle. So if someone doesn't have a container, I think God (or whatever you want to think of it as) is thinking, "This person can't handle a lot, so I'm not going to give them a lot to deal with." On the other hand, if someone does create a strong container, the way that I imagine it, God might be saying, "They've got a better handle on things. Now I can throw something juicy at him!"

This seems true in my own life. At times in the past when I would start practicing more intently, I'd suffer a major catastrophe in my life. I realize this isn't the most attractive endorsement for practice, but I should add that these sorts of things happened *before* I took the slow, kaizen approach. I would abruptly begin to meditate for two to three hours a day after not meditating at all for three to four months. So during those three to four months of non-meditation, no doubt things piled up inside my psyche, then I'd open the floodgates with two to three hour meditation sessions for weeks on end!

So, a three-breath container is good. I don't think God (or whoever) will be impressed to the point of saying, "I'm going to give this person a major health crisis now!" (Disclaimer: I don't think God actually works like this, but hopefully it helps make my point.) In short, the stronger the container, the deeper I've been able to go within during my practice, which is to say, I can touch into and ultimately release deeply-held energies. I'm able to withstand strong emotions and begin to work with them in a skillful manner, whereas ten to twenty years ago, these same strong emotions might have obliterated my psyche.

Also, the deeper I can go into these energies—including anger, rage, seemingly interminable anxiety, abject loneliness, utter depression; yes, these really "juicy" ones—the more consciously I can bring them up during my practice. Usually, when there's a strong charge of energy behind an emotion, a gift is in there, an insight, some potential for profound transformation, often proportional to the degree of the charge itself. [8]

In this way, if one doesn't have a container, there isn't a real chance for self-transformation, at least not with any self-reliance. To then have one's own container—even if it's just three breaths—allows for

---

[8] If interested, you might consider reading my other books, *The Gifts that Lie Hidden within Difficult Emotions*.

something meaningful and wondrous to start happening.

Rituals

Another word for a temporal container is a ritual. Consider a religion like Catholicism, which is chock full of rituals. Although they can be a deterrent for genuine inner inquiry when engaged in mindlessly, rituals do have a place in spiritual practice. They create structure, and thus, a container. In almost all spiritual practices, there are rituals or structures that act as containers and allow for psychic energy to be held within.

If you went to a Catholic mass, and everyone started free-form dancing, it would upset most participants, not just for social reasons, but due to a loss of structure. It would be the same if an Alcoholics Anonymous meeting suddenly consisted of an hour-long lecture on Postmodern French literature, or if there was an all-night rave with various hallucinogens at a Buddhist meditation retreat. It throws off our expectations of what these things mean, but also throws off the ritualistic elements of each gathering. When we lose structures and rituals, *we aren't able to settle in the same way.*

This settling is a large part of what makes meditation attractive as well as deepening. In settling, we can begin to delve beneath the surface and do some real work. So when it comes to creating a meditation practice, approaching it as the creation of a container or ritual can be helpful. One way in which to think of this temporal container is in terms of a beginning, middle and end.

For now, your practice consists of awareness of posture and three breaths. The plan for the next few weeks, starting with this one, is to install a beginning piece, then an end piece, and finally, a middle piece. On one hand, we can say we already have in place the middle piece, the three breaths, so it's the beginning and the end pieces that I'll suggest we add for the next few weeks to our already-existing three-breath practice. We'll start with the beginning, which we do by evoking bodhicitta, sometimes referred to as "raising bodhicitta" or "invoking bodhicitta."

In my own practice, I normally take a seat on my cushion, take a relaxed upright posture, and then take some time to relax in that position. I'm a bit on the slow side at times, so this might take a few minutes, but for the most, I think a few seconds is enough. Finally, I invoke bodhicitta.

So how is that done?

In exactly the same way you did at the beginning of this book, and hopefully, as you're doing each time you pick it up to read. You can check in with your *actual* motivations for practicing in an honest way, and from there, simply extend it (if necessary) so it includes an intention to become more awake and open for the sake of benefiting all beings. Or, if you're so inclined, you can do it as a simple prayer, such as "God, bless this session I'm about to have so that I may become more present and open so that I might be of greater benefit to all beings." In this way, we touch into bodhicitta, or some sense of a growth orientation combined with an altruistic intention.

The traditional phrasing, and the one I use regularly, is, "May I attain enlightenment for the benefit of all beings." Enlightenment itself may seem lofty, but if you're in the mood, why not aim high? If it's discouraging, then just intend for more presence and openness. But there's a lot of power in repetition. In the beginning, I considered enlightenment way off in some other reality, as in utterly impossible. Now, not as much (at least on good days). I attribute this to the power of repetition. (But also, I could be delusional.) On my not-so-good days, it feels like way too much. On those days, I think something more like, "Through today's practice, maybe I can grow a little bit so that my capacity to help others is increased by just a little bit?" It's a small sentiment that's more heartfelt for me on such low-energy days.

The idea is to *touch* the thought, and when we touch it, we're infusing that intention into our practice. This has a different feel than simply taking note of one's posture and counting the breaths. There's a sense of purpose that includes more than concern simply for one's own welfare. Instead of *just* sitting and getting relaxed and peaceful, we're also thinking of and sitting for others. We're setting a clear aim for growth, clarity, awakeness, and so on, for the benefit of all beings.

There's a lot of power and blessing in beginning a meditation practice with the raising of bodhicitta. Some schools of Dharma would say it's the most important part of a practice. You don't need to mean it always, as if you're going to become the next Buddha (someone will probably reprimand me for saying that, but oh well). Just touching the intention is important. In other words, simply grazing the intention of growth and increased capacity to help others is what's important for now.

—Week two

For the upcoming week, I suggest the following practice (or container).   (Suggested time ranges for each parts are in parentheses.):

1. Take a seat and go through the posture so it's relaxed and upright. (10 - 30 seconds.)

2. Ask yourself, "What are my actual motivations for practicing?" See what arises. Even if it's something like, "So I can be cool and out-spiritualize everyone around me," don't beat yourself up over it. Just notice it and maybe laugh if it's funny to you. Then ask yourself, "How can I extend it to include both a sense of growth or self-transformation as well as consideration of others?"

    Maybe for you it will sound something like, "I suppose out-spiritualizing others isn't the most important thing, but I want to slowly move toward becoming genuinely spiritual and humble, and eventually maybe I can help others in a meaningful way through this practice." Or maybe it sounds more like, "If I can become a bit more settled over time, I couldn't ask for anything more, actually. It would give me a peace I'm missing in my life. From there, I could be more patient, understanding and loving toward others. I wish that this practice moves me in this direction, however slightly." (10 - 60 seconds.)

3. Take *six* conscious breaths, settling with each breath. (One minute.)

That's the practice for now! It should take less than two to three minutes. I hope you already picked a regular time and location for this. It may be easy for you now, but we'll slowly grow the container from week to week, which is part of the rationale for spending the first few weeks simply training ourselves to show up on the cushion or chair at a regular time in a regular location. As I've mentioned before, just taking that seat is oftentimes the hardest part of meditation. We want to foster and nurture *that* particular habit for now.

Here is an additional suggestion for the week. Consider purchasing a small notebook to copy down ideas from this book, or any other, that support the idea of meditation. If you happen to be reading this on a Kindle, then that's convenient because all of your highlights will have been saved in its own file! You might print that out. We'll start using this notebook or file next week.

At this point, my suggestion is for you to spend the next week committing to this simple practice. If you're going to read out of this book, read over what you've read up until this point but not forward. After you've practiced for a week, start reading the next chapter.

Chapter 8: Karma and merit

It's said that meditating creates good karma.

There's a metaphor that says the life of a practitioner is akin to going *against the stream*, and by stream we mean the masses sleepwalking through this life, controlled by their passions (i.e., fixated desires, aversions, and delusions). By going against this stream of delusion and ignorance, one learns to relax and be more open, as well as becoming clearer in mind and heart. This relaxed and clear quality is the good karma, or part of it.

Although karma is a complicated concept, it's enough for our purposes to think of good karma as that which allows the mind and heart to become relaxed and clear. Bad karma then, is that which takes away the relaxed and clear quality of mind and heart.

Another word for good karma is merit.

I've been to many meditation retreats where we meditate twelve to fifteen hours a day for eight or nine days straight, or even up to two weeks, and I would somehow manage to enter into intensely profound states. I would feel very open—very good karma, one could say—and then the retreat would end, and I would drive home. On the way home, I'd stop by a restaurant or store and everything would look profoundly vibrant and alive. It would feel as if everyone was treating me like a radiant child, and I would think, *Life is so open and wonderful.*

Then I'd continue driving, maybe get stuck in traffic, become frustrated and start thinking, *I'm losing my peaceful feeling.* Maybe when I got home, I'd get into some conflict or misunderstanding with my partner, and within a week, I'd be back to "normal," or where I had started, more or less.

Certainly feeling good doesn't equate with good karma, but part of good karma *can be* feeling at ease, and most of the profound sense of ease I inhabited during the retreat would be gone within a week, even after all the arduous effort from the week prior. It's not that I turned into a ball of stress in a week, but more that whatever gains I seemingly made at the retreat were now gone. I still carried some of the ideas and insights, in addition to greater stamina around my sitting practice, but not the actual experience of feeling open from deep within my being. Sometimes I felt that much of the merit was wasted.

I've talked a bit about a formal meditation practice being a temporal container, and to think of it as having a beginning, middle, and end. These three parts structure our practice. In the section for week two, you began implementing the beginning portion of this container by invoking an altruistic motivation, akin to bodhicitta, if not bodhicitta itself. For this week, I'd like to focus on how to close a practice.

In some Buddhist traditions, a common way of ending a practice session is to offer the merit of our practice to all beings—that is, we offer up that clear, open quality of being to others. We can intend this, or we can offer it in some prayer-like form, whichever works better for each of us. A common phrasing is something like, *I offer the merit (good karma) of this practice to all beings so that they may attain enlightenment (ultimate happiness).*

When we've practiced, we've created a sense of openness or good karma, and we don't want to hold onto it only for ourselves. This doesn't mesh well with our original intention of bodhicitta, the altruistic motivation of practicing so that we can become more awake for others.

When I practiced meditation at these retreats, I wanted to hold onto the peace and openness afterwards. If I'm being completely honest with myself, I would say I wanted to hold onto the peace and open-ness *for myself.*

But now when I practice, I might still become peace-ful, yet at the end I offer whatever good that's come of the practice, including this open quality of being, to *all* beings. I make a conscious intent that the good quality goes outward from myself and that I don't hold onto it for myself. I think of it like this, *Okay, I've done some inner work, and there's some good that's gonna come out of this. Let me now send that good out to everyone else. I don't need to hold onto it for myself. My pleasure in all of this is that I get to do the work that I'm meant to be doing.* Or some-thing along those lines.

I find this freeing. I'm no longer holding onto a "re-sult" of my practice for myself. I still want to live in a dignified and virtuous way outside of my formal practice, but if someone bops me on the head, I'm not thinking, *Hey, I just practiced meditation! Some-thing like this shouldn't be happening to me!* Ridicu-lous as this may sound to some, I used to think things like this after a session, that instead, cool and won-drous things should be happening to me. Looking back, it was an awful pressure to put upon my prac-tice.

Now if someone were to karate-chop me on the head, I would just react, *Ow!* or *What the hell?!* But I wouldn't be thinking that my practice should have protected me from it. I don't want to put that kind of expectation or self-seeking agenda on my practice. The idea is that I want to be able to keep practicing daily, and the fewer undue and unrealistic expectations I put on meditation practice, the more likely I am to return to it.

Coming back to the container idea, we can think of it as *sealing* the practice on both ends, front and back. We seal it from the front end with the raising of bodhicitta, and on the back end with the dedication of merit. That is, we offer this good karma. We don't hold onto it for ourselves. Another way to say this is that we don't defile or taint our practice with a preponderance of self, or our egoistic agenda. We want to have as little of our self-driven agenda in practice if we want our practice to sustain itself. The more that the self insinuates itself into practice, the more tense it can become, for that's the nature of ego—tension.

If we engage in the sealing on both ends, at least there's some relief from the ego in the beginning with bodhicitta—again, even just touching it—and at the end with dedication of merit. Even if it's not entirely heartfelt, just the intention to touch into it can be enough. In time, it can grow and become more heartfelt.

This is how we continue to build the ritual or container of a formal meditation practice. We touch into the two-fold intention of bodhicitta at the beginning, then we engage in meditation in the middle, and at the end, recognizing that there's merit involved in our efforts, we offer it to all beings so that they can attain the deepest and most profound form of happiness.

It's been my experience and conviction, that this is how we begin to build a sustainable practice. On a personal level, it feels relatively clean of ego-grasping, and it's one of the few things in my life that *consistently* feels this way, and as a result, has become a source from which the rest of my life can begin to feel similarly.

—Week three

For this week, my suggestion for practice is outlined below. Note that I've chosen to structure the practice in terms of preliminary steps, followed by a beginning, middle, and end.

Preliminary:

1. Hopefully, you've settled upon a *set* time and place.

2. Just as with last week, take a relaxed and upright posture in your seat and allow yourself to settle in a bit.

Beginning:

3. Raise bodhicitta. That is, touch into a motivation that's true for you, that entails inner or personal growth and your impact upon others.

Middle:

4. Instead of taking three breaths, I'm going to suggest using a timer from this point forward. For this week, set the timer for one minute. This is *after* invoking bodhicitta.

   There "are a number of free apps available for your phone under "mindfulness bell" or meditation timer." If you can download one, set it for one minute. If you don't want to use your phone, you can simply purchase a timer at the store or online.

   Although I've already talked about meditation techniques, or what to do with one's mind during the "middle" portion of our practice—and there are many others—I want to share one other way of spending your time in meditation. This is a simple thing that I sometimes do informally, especially when I'm out and about, such as at a doctor's office or while shopping, or I sometimes do this when I'm out in nature as well. All this method entails is the following: *you simply set an intention to be present on a regular interval.*

   When I set an intention to be present at the top of my practice, this might result in me paying attention to my visual surroundings in the moment. Or my mind might become more aware of the surrounding sounds. [9] A more traditional

---

[9] One of the benefits of meditation is that one can turn anything into an excuse for meditation. For example, when I am writing

manner of being present is to attune to whatever bodily sensations avail themselves to my awareness. Maybe it's the sensation of my chest expanding on an in-breath or a "cool" sensation in my nostrils as my breath moves in and out.

Then, a few seconds later, I reset the intention of being present, and I'm back to being aware of my sensory input in the moment. And again a few seconds later, I reset the intention, and so on and so forth.

There are two things worth noting here. One has to do with this idea of becoming present. I'm confident that if you're reading this book, you already know the importance or the "power" of now, or of being present in the moment, so I won't elaborate upon that here. What I will mention is this: most of us fail to live in the present moment for long stretches at a time, and yet, when we sit down for meditation we're suddenly striving to be present. There's often a huge discrepancy between the two, and I think this difference can make meditation daunting for some. In light of this, I'd like to offer encouragement.

---

and the next door neighbor's dog is barking loudly enough for the cries to pierce into me, it's a bit of an annoyance. And yet, during meditation, I can choose to use that exact sound, as well as my honest response to that sound, as the objects of my meditation to bring me into the present moment.

Consider the graph below. The horizontal axis stands for time, so as we move from left to right, we're moving across time. That same axis also represents the present moment and the curvy line is our mind in its usual state, for most of us. Notice that the curvy line is mostly off the horizontal axis, meaning our minds are hardly ever present. Some of us are constantly regretting or reconsidering the past, while others of us are planning or fearing the future, or some combination of the two.

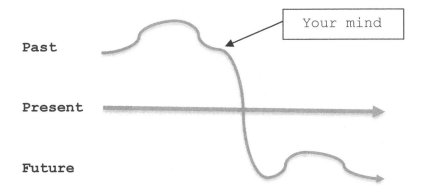

Some beginners to meditation might think of meditation as trying to bring their minds *flat onto* the present moment, an approach that contains within it a subtle aggression against one's everyday self in striving for such presence.

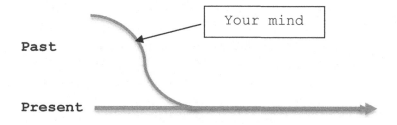

Past

Present

Future

In my experience, as well as with others I have worked with, there is a much gentler way to approach this. Rather than *coercing* our minds into the present moment, we can approach meditation more as the act of *touching* into the present moment on a regular basis. Notice how in the graph below, our commitment isn't to laying our minds *flat* onto the present moment, but to touching it regularly though our intention of doing so.

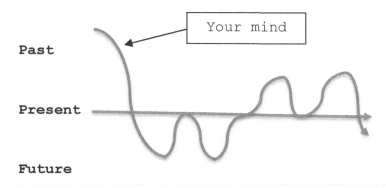

Past

Present

Future

As we continue to do this, the mind gradually settles closer and closer to the present. It begins to relax into it.

Although we don't get a perfect up-and-down "sine wave" (since we're not switching off into past and future in a neat and orderly way after each encounter with the present moment), you might think of meditation as a sine wave if it helps you with this gentler approach of touching into the moment.

So we set and reset our intention to be present. At this point, since you're meditating for one minute, you might just do it two or three times in your session, maybe every twenty or thirty seconds. There's no point in being anxious about it. If you do it just once, it might be enough. If you do it ten times, that might be too much right now.

The second thing I want to point to has to do with how we become present once the intention is set. Our minds have a tendency to become lost in thought, taking us out of the present moment. *But our senses bring us back into the moment.* If you think about it, it's impossible to see, listen, feel, smell, or taste some outer object anywhere but in the present moment.

For example, if you sit by a stream and set the intention to listen to the sound of it for a few seconds, *your listening will occur in the present moment.* Your mind may wander off into the future as in "Oooh, this is so cool, I want to come here again tomorrow." Or it may go off into the past as in, "That sound I just heard, it's so reminiscent of a piece of music I've heard before. Why haven't I done this kind of thing more often in my life?"

And yet, the listening itself happens in the moment.

When I listen to something like a stream, it's the same old quasi-sine wave phenomenon. *I'm regularly touching into the act of listening where I hear the actual sounds and my mind is aligned with the hearing aspect of my experience.* But a lot of it is that I'm thinking also, about how much I like the sound, how it makes me feel, about some girl I just met, or how I can package this into something that will make me money. And the list goes on and on.

The same can be said of seeing. When I set my intention to be present, sometimes I focus on my visual perception, and I notice color, texture, shape, light and shade, space, lines and angles more acutely. It's easy for someone like me to get caught up in a desire for systematization of visual phenomenon, such as "Is color more primal than shape?" I can get lost in thought for anywhere from a few seconds to a few minutes. But during meditation, I'll reset my intention to become present and snap myself out of the reverie of thought and back into the visual domain of lived experience.

Another often-used sense is that of tactile sensation, particularly around the movement caused by the breath. We may focus our minds upon the sensation of our stomachs moving up and down with the breath, or we may notice how the breath feels as it moves through our throats or nostrils. When we pay attention to the sensation itself—and not analyze or pontificate over it—our minds anchor into the present. In this way, we begin to touch into the present moment through our senses.

I haven't said much about smell or taste, and yet I don't think it's an accident that we have the saying, "Stop and smell the roses." In smelling, we're brought into the moment, out of the whirlwind of activity and accomplishment many of us can get wrapped up in. At the same time, I find it difficult to use the olfactory senses during formal meditation, mainly because the smells are too subtle for me to detect most of the time.

Similarly with taste, we generally don't eat things while meditating formally. On the other hand, we can bring meditation into the act of eating. There are entire books written on this subject, but that's beyond the scope of this book.[10]

In summary, I've offered an alternative method to meditation here, which involves setting and resetting the intention to being present, and once that intention is set, utilizing one of the senses (or sensory lived experiences) to do so. Try it out and see how it works for you.

5. Once the minute has passed, leaf through your notebook of notes (from week 2). Your eyes and mind might alight on just one passage, or you might read a few. The idea is that you want your mind to settle upon these ideas. You want to expose yourself to these ideas repeatedly, in the weeks, months, and years to come. You could do this for as short as a few seconds, and as long as three or four minutes.

Ending:

6. At this point, consider the merit of what you've just accomplished. Think of its value. Even if you think, *this is hardly anything, just a drop in the bucket,* that's still one drop of value. Try to recognize how wonderful it is that you actually

---

[10] One can type in "mindfulness" and "eating" into a search engine such as google or amazon and find a plethora of sources on this topic.

took a seat and tried to meditate and center yourself into the present moment. Think of how much merit it takes for someone to go against the grain of everyday living to take a few conscious breaths and nothing more. Think of all the days you've lived when you weren't able to sit quietly without distraction for even a minute. If you really think about it, it's an extraordinary thing. Many people run around non-stop, and you've taken a few minutes just to be, or attempted just to be.

Think of your practice session as being of tremendous value, and then, imagine offering up that value for the happiness and health of all beings. If you like, use a phrase such as, "By the merit of this practice, may all beings attain enlightenment" or "Whatever value I've generated through this practice, I offer for the benefit of all beings." Or you might come up with your own phrase or prayer. In this way, your practice is beginning to hold a structure—one that includes others.

Chapter 9: Refuge

I want to begin this section by first addressing the readers who might carry a strongly charged *anti*-theistic bent. My intent here isn't to promote theism, by any means, but I am going to advocate on behalf of the concept or experience of the *sacred* or *spiritual*. I'm of the mind that what we term the "sacred" or "spiritual" is independent of the divine. That is, one can have a sense of the sacred/spiritual without requiring a notion of God or a deity. I also happen to believe that what many call the "divine," is nothing more than an experience of the sacred. In other words, the two words are interchangeable for some and distinct for others.

For these reasons, I will more often use the word "sacred" throughout this chapter, but because it makes for poor writing to keep using the same word repeatedly, I will also replace it with the word "divine" and "spiritual" (I have my own prejudice against the latter term, mostly from overuse). Part of this has to do with my own bias, which is that I hold these words closely together. But if you do not, I hope you will mentally replace my use of the word "divine" with "sacred," "spiritual," or some other word that is more palatable to you.

I want to make a secondary disclaimer in the spirit of transparency. I have no intention of trying to convert anyone to Buddhism, but because my background is steeped in Buddhism, and it's the primary perspective with which I'm most familiar, I'll be using metaphors and images from that tradition to help explain the concept of *refuge*, which I consider to be larger than Buddhism.

My intent in this chapter is to start within the context of Buddhism to lay out some ideas. Then I'll expand outwardly—that is, generalize the ideas—so that readers outside of Buddhism might find a way to connect and resonate with what I think of as a powerful set of concepts and practices that will support a robust meditation practice, regardless of one's belief system.

As a reminder, my main motivation here is to help you to build a *container* of a daily practice. I've talked about this temporal container as having a beginning, middle, and end. For the beginning, there is the twofold intention of relative bodhicitta of having compassion for others, and out of that compassion, wanting to practice toward some self-transformation (which for Buddhists would end in enlightenment). We contact this intention within ourselves to set the stage for our practice. Then we practice in the middle, which we'll build upon once the beginning and end pieces are set in place. And at the end, we dedicate the merit, or the value created through the practice, for all beings. This is how we hold the container of practice.

In this section, I'll add to the beginning of the container with the practice of refuge, which in my view is one of the most important pieces to our container. But before getting to refuge, I want to mention the Three Jewels or Roots: the Buddha, the Dharma, and the Sangha.

For some Buddhists, the Buddha is the *human being* who became enlightened, the historical figure. For others, the Buddha is held as an omniscient being, much like a deity. And for others, the Buddha is representative of the ultimate potential within each of us, or taken further, as bodhicitta itself—that is, Buddha is synonymous with the state of being that is enlightened, the infinite compassion and utter clarity and spaciousness of mind that sees through all illusory aspects of reality. Naturally, all three ways of holding the "Buddha" can be held simultaneously as well.

The Dharma is the Buddha's teachings, what he taught others so they could gain enlightenment. It's considered that what he *knew* was significantly more vast than what he *taught*. The understanding is that not everything was integral to enlightenment. So for some Buddhists, the Dharma is this set of teachings. For others, it's the path laid out by the teachings. And yet for others, because that path leads to ultimate knowing and enlightenment, Dharma is held as the state of enlightened being, again, which is bodhicitta. As with the Buddha, the Dharma can be held simultaneously in these different ways.

The Sangha is the group of persons who practice the teachings of the Buddha and follow the path as laid out in the Dharma. I liken this to the Christian or Western notion of congregation or fellowship. The word "Sangha" is sometimes qualified with an adjective, as in the "ordained Sangha" and the "non-ordained Sangha," the former being the congregation of ordained monks and nuns, and the latter being the lay practitioners.

Sometimes there will be reference to the "Supreme Sangha." You may have come across deities or bodhisattvas such as Red Tara, Green Tara, Avalokiteshvara, Medicine Buddha, Padmasambhava, and so on. These are considered enlightened beings or enlightened bodhisattvas. When we refer to the Supreme Sangha, it is usually in reference to this assembly of enlightened beings, which includes the Buddha himself. [11] But it doesn't include ordinary

---

[11] The Supreme Sangha is a motley crew of beings, some of whom are historical beings, and others who are more mythical in nature. Ultimately, each of these enlightened beings is considered a reflection of the one *Shakyamuni* Buddha.

folks like you and me, as well as most monks and nuns who are considered ordinary, or still not fully enlightened.

What Does it Mean to Take Refuge in the Three Jewels?

At the very beginning of a Buddhist meditation retreat (in the Theravada tradition), the retreat leader will often announce, "I would like to lead you in the refuge chant. You are welcome to join. And if not, you're welcome just to be silent." The chant will often be done in Pali (see below). Then, it will be followed in English.

Pali:
Buddham Saranam Gacchâmi.
Dhammam Saranam Gacchâmi.
Sangham Saranam Gacchâmi.
Dutiyampi Buddham Saranam Gacchâmi.
Dutiyampi Dhammam Saranam Gacchâmi.
Dutiyampi Sangham Saranam Gacchâmi.
Tatiyampi Buddham Saranam Gacchâmi.
Tatiyampi Dhammam Saranam Gacchâmi.
Tatiyampi Sangham Saranam Gacchâmi.

English:
I go for refuge in the Buddha.
I go for refuge in the Dhamma.
I go for refuge in the Sangha.
For the second time, I go for refuge in the Buddha.
For the second time, I go for refuge in the Dhamma.

For the second time, I go for refuge in the Sangha.
For the third time, I go for refuge in the Buddha.
For the third time, I go for refuge in the Dhamma
For the third time, I go for refuge in the Sangha. [12]

This is more or less a ritual where *the intent behind it is to connect with a source of support or power, that is stable, profound and can aide in the meditative retreat journey that one is about to embark upon.*

When we say we are taking refuge in the Buddha, it depends upon how we hold the Buddha. If we hold him as the historical figure, then we might think, "Yes, he was a wise man, and so I'm going to put my faith and confidence in him even though I don't know him personally." If we hold the Buddha similarly to how some Christians might hold God or Jesus, then refuge in the Buddha would be akin to seeking salvation in God or Jesus. If we hold him more as our own inner potential for complete transformation, then our refuge is more like a psychological refuge. In this case, we're not taking refuge in

---

[12] On a technical note, the Sangha in this context is typically meant to include all practitioners. And yet, if one takes refuge in the Supreme Sangha (as is more often done in the Tibetan tradition), then one is taking refuge only in those enlightened beings as explained earlier, and not in the ordinary folks who are sitting around us. I don't believe there's a "right way," so much as a way that resonates for oneself at a particular point in one's journey.

the man who lived 2,500 years ago so much as in our own ultimate potential. And if we hold the Buddha more as the essence of his heart and mind—that is, his infinite compassion and utter clarity to see through the illusory nature of reality, or simply, relative and absolute bodhicitta—then we rest into bodhicitta itself.

When we take refuge in the Dharma, if we hold the Dharma as the teachings themselves, then we might think, "These are wonderful and beautiful teachings, and they seem to hold some sacred or healing power, so I'm going to rest my faith or confidence in that." If we hold the Dharma more as the path laid out by those teachings, then that's what we're putting our faith into, and we begin bringing our lives into alignment with that path. And if we consider the endpoint of Dharma as the essence of Dharma, then we rest into that endpoint, which again is nothing other than bodhicitta. Dzongsar Khyentse Rinpoche, a prominent Buddhist Teacher in the Tibetan tradition, has written that the point of Dharma is to arrive at emptiness—or again, bodhicitta—and once one arrives at that, one doesn't need the Dharma. It's a rather strong position, I think, but it speaks to this last view of holding Dharma.

With regards to Sangha, if you hold the Sangha as the actual people or Buddhas, depending upon whether you're taking refuge in the Sangha or the Supreme Sangha, you're putting your confidence in the congregation of all practitioners or else the Buddhas and bodhisattvas, respectively. On the other hand, if you hold the Sangha as the ultimate potential within each of the practitioners, then you're resting into that quality within others. It's similar to the yogic notion of *namaste,* as in "The sacred in me honors the sacred in you." And if we're clear that the ultimate potential of all beings is bodhicitta itself, then to take refuge in the Sangha can mean to rest into bodhicitta, just as with the previous two.

In beginning one's practice, I've suggested that we try to contact or invoke a natural compassion for others and from that, a desire to practice toward greater self-transformation. When we bring it up, we can take refuge in this quality of being. If you pay close attention, you might notice there's an unbounded, infinite quality to this state of being. From this perspective, you don't need a Buddha outside of you, and you don't even need a Buddha inside. That *is* the Buddha. There's no other Buddha other than bodhicitta.

My own relationship to refuge is dependent upon my state of mind, which like many of us, tends to fluctuate. Sometimes I'm able to settle into bodhicitta. At other times, my mind is restless and busy, and it's challenging even to graze bodhicitta. But I can still acknowledge that the historical Buddha was likely a wise and kind man, that his teachings make a lot of sense, and in turn, put my confidence in that. For me, this is better than no refuge at all, when I can't

connect to some psychological idea called my ultimate potential, much less a tangible experience of
bodhicitta.

In this way, I consider it beneficial to have fluid in-
terpretations of the three jewels. These different
ways of holding the three jewels then allow me different entry points dependent upon my state of
mind. I can enter into some relationship with them
according to my current state or capacity, which can
waver day to day, even minute to minute.

The Purpose of Refuge

The purpose of refuge is to connect to a source of
support for one's endeavors in the spiritual
life. Here, I'd like to offer a quick analogy.

Imagine that you live in a house somewhere, and
your next-door neighbors are the Buddha and Jesus. One day you decide to go on an adventure, such
as a journey around the world. You have a number
of options in this scenario. You could simply depart
on your adventure and think, "I'm glad I have these
great neighbors. They'll probably do a good job
watching out for my house." Most of us would more
likely walk over to their places before embarking on
our long journey and say, "Jesus, I know that you're a
great man. Some would even call you godly. Can
you bless me on my journey?" Next, we'd go to the
Buddha and say, "I know who you are also. Jesus,

next door, already offered me some blessings.
Would you bless me also?"

I think many of us would do something like that before embarking on a potentially arduous journey (assuming that we don't allow them to talk us into
staying there and listening to their teachings and following them around instead).

Refuge is about making contact with some profound,
infinite source of inspiration, support, and/or
love. When we practice meditation, even for just one
minute, we're embarking on an internal journey. Why wouldn't we turn to a source of blessing
beforehand? This is the spirit of refuge.

Even in a simple act like a prayer, there is something
similar going on. As I've mentioned, I regularly pray
to what might be considered a Christian God, of
sorts. Supposing I wanted a new car, not that that's
what I've ever prayed for but for the sake of example,
suppose I did. I would never do it like this, "Yo,
give me a new car!" or "Hey, I want a new car!" Instead, I would say (in a more settled voice), "God,
please provide for me a new car," or maybe, "God, I
would really love a new car," or else, "God, if it be
Thy Will, I really need a new car." I would call out
His name. I wouldn't start the prayer with "Dude" or
"Hey, man." And if I was serious, I might start instead with "Lord Jesus Christ, son of God... uh, I
need a car please."

In other words, there's a power to how to we address who we're praying to.

For me, there's a difference in uttering the words "Jesus..." vs "Lord Jesus Christ..." There's a power I feel in saying the *full* name, even adding "son of God." I'm elevating Him and connecting to Him, and my heart comes along for the ride (of the prayer). In this way, I much prefer addressing traditional forms of divinity with as much honorifics as I can. It somehow quiets the tone of my address.

Even with a deity such as Krishna, I strongly prefer saying or thinking something like, "Dear sweet Lord Krishna." There's a softening to me about it, versus simply saying "Lord Krishna." The "dear" and "sweet," in fact sweeten and add a devoted, tender quality to the address.

Likewise in chants, the way one calls out the deities can be important. *It has to do with how it allows the heart to connect.* It can make tender and/or intensify the connection. And this is how I hold refuge. It's connecting into the sacred through some manifested form of it.

The Nuts and Bolts of Refuge for Me

Even though I've already scattered a lot of auto-biographical details throughout this book, in this section I want to share specifics of how *I* engage in and hold refuge.

Insofar as speech is concerned, I either say out loud
or quietly in my mind, "In the Buddha, the Dharma,
and the Supreme Sangha, I take refuge until enlightenment." This is pretty standard for some Buddhist
lineages. As I say this, I imagine the meaning of
each of the words, particularly, each of the Three
Jewels. I recognize that for someone such as myself,
it's a long road to enlightenment, but until that point,
I'll be turning to the Three Jewels as a source of
strength, as a source of power, and a source of inspiration. I'm essentially asking for their support.

Sometimes though, I will also do this same refuge
chant in Tibetan:

Sangye choe dang tsok kyi chok nam la
Jang chup bar du dak ni kyap su chi

As I chant these Tibetan words, I usually think the
English equivalent, although it can be tricky when
I'm not concentrating well. The reason why I chant
the Tibetan is because it's been chanted by millions
of people, for some time now. There's a lot of consciousness attached to that particular configuration of
sounds, just as with many of the mantras in the East,
such as *om mani padme hung,* the mantra for Avalokiteshvara.

So when I incant the refuge chant, my sense is that
I'm connecting to a large flow of consciousness that
surrounds that specific pattern of sounds. Sometimes

I want that connection, whereas in English it's more about connecting to the meaning of the words, which has great value in its own right. (With the Tibetan chanting, this also offers another way to think of connecting to the Sangha, as one is joining in with all the others who have chanted this same set of syllables with a similar intent.)

Intermediary to the Divine

Although mystics and practitioners of many traditions including Buddhism say that the ultimate reality is one of nondualism, I think it's useful to talk dualistically since most of us live within dualistic consciousness much of the time. So that's what I'm going to do here to try to expand upon the idea of refuge, beyond Buddhism and toward a general spirituality.

Imagine, if you will, that there's the divine world and the ordinary world, or divine and ordinary reality. Most of us live in what we think of as ordinary consciousness, and have a notion of there being a divine or sacred reality that we're trying to make contact with from our ordinary state. For some spiritual seekers, this could be one way of describing the heart of their spiritual endeavor. They're trying to become one with *the* Divine. [13]

---

[13] Once such a person becomes "one with the Divine," they experience that *all* is divine, that it always was divine and always will be. But as long as there's the frame of mind that something

What are the different ways or forms in which we could connect with this divine?

Up until the age of 25, much of my so-called contact with the divine or sacred was through what I would consider a conceptual or mental connection. That is, I had ideas and concepts about it. I referred to it as "Higher Power," and I could tell you many facets of this Higher Power, but that was about it.

And then, when I was about 25, I met a Christian woman. At the time, I happened to have a strong disdain for Christianity. I don't have it now, but I did then. But it turned out that I liked this Christian woman very much. I ended up marrying her—although when I first found out about her religious beliefs, I remember thinking, "Why is this happening to me?"

In the beginning of our relationship, I was rather immature and unpleasant around this issue. One time we were talking, and I was questioning the validity of her views saying things like, "You believe in your God floating around in the sky! What kind of nonsense is this? And what, is Jesus smiling up in the

---

"over there" is good and divine, and something here is not divine, there's dualism. Thus, we end up living in this dualistic reality.

sky somewhere?" She looked at me, completely un-guarded, rested her palms on her heart and said, "Je-sus is in here." When she said that, I *knew*. In that moment, I woke up from a level of my own igno-rance. I realized that whatever *conceptualization* I had of the divine, from that point forward it wasn't going to be good enough.

Up until that point, this "Higher Power" was sort of "out there"—mostly in the sky if I was being honest with myself. In other words, I was the one being silly in the same way I had accused her of being. I knew people who used the acronym G.O.D. for "good orderly direction." That's what it was like for me; there was no genuine *heartfelt* connec-tion. Mostly mental or conceptual, although tinged with some intuitive element. It was more like, "Yeah, good orderly direction. God is basically a heuristic for what I'm supposed to do! You know, intuition."

After that incident with this person who would be-come my wife, I realized I had based my spirituality upon something other than what was in my heart. When she told me that Jesus was in her heart, she put up a mirror of what was possible instead of the dry, conceptual, "try to do the right thing" and ul-timately unrelaxed attitude I had toward the sacred and the divine. I knew then, that whatever concepts I had about the divine, I would need to let them go. I would instead look for something within my heart.

She became my model. I tossed aside most of what I knew about spirituality up to that point, and began looking around more carefully. I spoke with people about this, listened to them, read books, until one day someone mentioned a name I had heard before, and my heart opened. I knew at that moment that it was going to be my primary contact point to the divine, an intermediary.

I believe that Jesus is that person to many in the West. He says, "Through me, you can know God." In other words, through him, you can know the divine. But to me, Jesus was just a person. He wasn't my contact point then, although I consider him a contact point for me now. But not the one and only. (Sorry Christians!)

At that time and for the longest time, the manifestation or intermediary to the sacred for me was Avalokiteshvara, in particular, "Quan Yin"—the Chinese female incarnation of Avalokiteshvara. When I spoke her name or simply turned my mind toward her, my heart opened. Immediately. So I knew.

I also knew that the word "Higher Power" was no longer the best descriptor because it wasn't about power, but more about a presence. It also wasn't higher than me but within. So, it was more like an "inner presence." I didn't tell anyone about this other than my wife, but I knew it was how I could and would connect to the Great Mystery.

I share this here to offer a generalized image of what taking refuge can mean, that it's about a heartfelt or heart connection to some aspect of the sacred. What I found was that when my so-called connection was primarily conceptual or mental in nature, it was of little help during difficult emotional times. It was primarily *ideas*. But with the heart connections— many more that I've established and deepened since that beginning—they are ever present. Regardless of my mental or emotional state—depression, loneliness, anger, anxiety, and so on—the connections are there, and somehow, they offer comfort as well as strength. In fact, one of my primary endeavors in this life turns out to be strengthening these connections and going about my life with that sense of connectedness, so that my actions, speech and thoughts might come from a place of intrinsic connection rather than separation.

When I speak of finding an intermediary to the sacred, I don't mean to suggest that one need find an already-established "religious" form for it. For some people, it might simply be Nature Herself, or maybe peering at the stars. For others, it could be in the innocence of animals or children. All these are still intermediaries. What matters, I believe, is that through these representations of that which we hold sacred, we're able to peer into the infinite and mysteriously profound, and that *the heart is intricately and intimately involved.*

And yet, I still believe that for most of us, there is added value in seeking out already-established visages of the divine, and "personalizing" them as one's own portals into the sacred. There are three reasons I can think of. The first has to do with the advantage of multiplicity and stems from the fact that we are all human beings, and most religions *at their core* are essentially creations of archetypes of our psyche. That is, there is bound to be a pre-existent form of a deity, or representation that is a good fit for us. There are so many traditions and lineages in so many cultures! I would find it hard to believe that one or a few couldn't be tracked down as a fit to one's current psyche if one was sincere and persistent in one's seeking. It can be a fun exercise as well, a cultural/spiritual exploration into different forms of the sacred that exist and have existed in our human history. The added value here is that one can expand the ways to connect into the divine. If you only have one door in, then you only have one way in. If you have ten doors in, you have more flexibility. Depending on your particular mood, perhaps the red door works better, or maybe the blue one does.

The second reason for the added value relates to a quote by Isaac Newton that I've long been fond of— *"If I have seen further, it is by standing on the shoulders of giants"* [Translated into Modern English]. In other words, we have many spiritual predecessors— sometimes called teachers, enlightened beings, saints, shamans, high priests and priestesses—many of whom conducted immense inner work to discover or create (depending upon your perspective) different representations *of* and *into* the sacred and divine. By finding what's already out there, we are essentially standing on the shoulders of these spiritual giants, reaping the advantages of their work and vision.

And the third reason relates to what I mentioned when explaining why I sometimes chant in Tibetan. While I might be able to contact the divine directly without any pre-established, agreed upon intermediaries, if I can do so through Avalokiteshvara, trickster coyote, Hanuman, Mother Mary—there are so many more traditions to consider—it's as if I'm connecting to a long tradition, that is, a long stream of consciousness of many other seekers. I am then no longer an individual stream, but *part of a lineage of blessings* that for me includes beings such the Buddha, Jesus, and so on. This feels powerful and real to me, not just in terms of the idea of it, but in my experience of it.

If you find an image that connects for you, you might read about it and learn other qualities associated with it. Maybe some of them are latent in you, and you realize, "I currently seem to be a manifestation of this quality or energy, and so perhaps these other aspects are a part of me as well." After all, these images or deities that are supposedly "out there" can also be understood to be archetypes within our own psyche.

For example, if I have a native connection to Green Tara, who is swift in action and quick to help, then the more I connect to this quality, the more able I might be to bring these qualities to bear within my own being. It can be a powerful experience to connect to some or many faces of divinity that are already existent. This is the power of tradition. [14] It is the power of entering a large river of blessings, as well as connecting to an immense historical and present community or Sangha, that constitutes this river of consciousness. In this way, the concept of taking refuge is about connecting to this larger source, like a river tumbling down from an authentic source.

Suppose you don't have a connection to any so-called "intermediaries" and would like to have one (or two or more)? In this case, the easiest thing to do is simply to ask. You could ask the universe or your psyche for some form, a particular configuration, a manifestation, an intermediary. Then, you have to be on the lookout, see where you're drawn, while also being patient with the process.

This means being open, not having preconceived ideas of how it should happen or show up in your life. It could happen in the most seemingly superficial or contrived manner. For example, you might just be drawn to how a particular deity has been etched by a particular artist, their facial expression,

_____

[14] Naturally, tradition can come with certain drawbacks as well, such as an over-emphasis on conservatism and control, but most of these can be obviated by critical thinking and questioning, in my view.

or the colors of their gown. It might even be that their name sounds like yours, or the name of your favorite aunt. Your attraction could also be to what they represent. In the end, I'm not sure it matters. If you're drawn to some representation of the divine, for one reason or another, then you might just trust that impulse. A lot of living intuitively is about learning to trust some inner impulse, no matter how seemingly shallow or profound it may seem to the rational mind.

A good sign, in my experience and opinion, is that your heart opens or softens upon the encounter.

But also, I think things can happen in unexpected ways. It may not always be a matter of straight-forward softening of the heart that gives the sign. One can also *forge* a connection through effort.

In one instance, I was drawn to a particular teacher, not to any deity. His presence and his teachings galvanized me in the way that I stood in this world. It just so happens this teacher was a Buddhist in the *Nyingma* tradition, and within that tradition, *Padmasambhava*[15] is a central figure next to the Buddha himself. So I was given a set of practices all aimed at essentially forging a deeper connection with Padmasambhava. For the longest time, I felt little to no

---

[15] Padmasambhava, or Guru Rinpoche, in Tibetan Buddhism is often described as the "second Buddha."

connection. I was mouthing mantras while doing prostrations and other related practices. But I did them because I respected my teacher enough, and I thought that if he felt they were worthwhile exercises, they likely were.

At some point—and it happened rather abruptly—I felt connected, or rather, *Padmasambhava felt real to me in my mind and my heart*. Once that happened, but not anytime before that moment, it was as if the connection had always been there, and had just been clouded over all this time. So, it didn't feel like a new connection so much as rediscovering an old one. I even began to think that maybe my karma was linked to Padmasambhava from long ago, and I had chosen my teacher so that I could be brought back to Padmasambhava himself, that all of the practices simply helped to remove the blockages that had been there to prevent the experience of connection. Or, this could be little more than a nice story to tell myself.

The larger point is that if we ask, something shows up, and from there, we can either further or re-establish a connection, where re-establishing involves assiduous effort that may not feel particularly connecting until the moment of reconnection.

Pragmatism

> "The test of a first-rate intelligence is the ability to hold two opposed ideas in mind at

the same time and still retain the ability to function." -- F. Scott Fitzgerald.

In case you're feeling uncomfortable with the idea of establishing a meditation practice centered upon deities and mythical beings that may have little to no historical reality— in other words, building a spiritual life upon "fantasy," as some might describe it— I want to assuage your concerns through a short discussion on the philosophical tradition of pragmatism.

Pragmatism doesn't concern itself so much with ontological truthfulness or goodness (as in, is such and such true in some absolute sense?), but rather, the pragmatic consequences of "truths," so to speak. In other words, it doesn't posit whether there is such a thing as *true* goodness or *true* badness that can be talked about outside of pragmatic outcome. What it does instead, is to evaluate ideas based upon their pragmatic value. Suppose there is a statement such as, "Treating others well is a good thing." A pragmatist will conduct a thought experiment that asks, "If this statement is taken as *true*, what is the actual outcome in how things play out?" After evaluating and thinking through the various possibilities, they will then do another thought experiment asking, "What if I were to accept this statement as being *false*. How do things play out then?"

Whichever outcome is *pragmatically* better in terms of the happiness of self and others will then determine whether the pragmatist wants to adopt the original statement as true or false, or good or bad.[16]

The real question then, with regards to these ethereal ideas such as deities (i.e., Avalokiteshvara, Red Tara, Krishna, the Buddha as an omniscient being, Jesus as God, and so on), is not whether they're historically or ontologically true or not, but rather, how will your life be informed by adopting the reality of these mythical beings?

In my own experience, when I considered the historical Buddha as described in the Pali Canon, which is that of a wise and liberated *human being*, I felt a certain quality of relationship toward the teacher and being that he was. But when I thought of the Buddha as *more* than just the man, as an emanation of a more infinite being, it opened my heart more. I had deeper inspiration to practice more engagedly, and a greater capacity to relax into my meditation practice, as well as in my daily life. I figured then that adopting the latter reality as true—which subsumes the former also—was a better pragmatic choice for me.

I may be wrong in terms of actual facts, but pragmatically the outcome was better. I felt more connected

---

[16] I have grossly oversimplified the epistemological outlook of pragmatism, but I hope to have captured the essence of it through the one example.

in my heart. This is to say that it's *pragmatically* true for me. I haven't compromised my modern intelligence by talking myself into believing some of these mythical beings are historical beings. I mostly see them as archetypes. But by holding them as real on some level, my practice is strengthened. I needn't collapse reality down to one or the other. It's possible to hold both the ontological as well as pragmatic truths concurrently, or I've found this true for myself.

The Buddha himself taught similarly—that is, pragmatically—when he said (paraphrased), "Try these ideas and see for yourself how they play out for you." I hope that you too will take on a pragmatic perspective in deciding whether to seek out, or uphold if already existent, your relationship to these various intermediaries that may or may not have existed historically.

A Quick Q&A from a Gathering:

Question: *I'm one of these people who has a very natural capacity to connect to the spiritual realm without an "intermediary," as you call it. At the same time, I feel a bit "orphaned" when I listen to you speak of these intermediaries. Could you speak to that?*

My response: I think it's wonderful that you have such a gift. So, no, you don't need one. I don't want you to take away from this that you actually need one to have a practice. Your refuge can simply be in the spiritual quality of experience that you're so easily able to touch.

But I still think there are advantages to these intermediaries. I'm speaking as someone who is like you. I may not need one, but I've seen advantages to cultivating relationships with these intermediaries that are a bit like cultivating different kinds of friendships in my life. I've already spoken of the value of multiplicity. Even if I were completely self-sufficient emotionally in my daily life, it's nice to have a friend or two. It's also nice to have many friends. That's my attitude toward these spiritual intermediaries.

Sometimes, I'm able to go straight there (without seeking out the help of an intermediary). Other times, I would rather have something more "embodied" (for lack of a better term) to work with. Different intermediaries are like different portals. It's nice to have ten portals, each fitting a different state of mind and mood. If I don't have any and rely only on my natural capacity, I have to work hard on further developing that natural capacity, and so it grows stronger. On the other hand, it can be discouraging when I would rather find a portal closer to my current state of consciousness.

I once attended an introductory massage therapy class. I never went any further with the training, but I remember one thing the instructor said, which was that massage is an intuitive art, but sometimes we're not entirely in tune with our intuition because something may be blocked. During those times it's good to have something to fall back upon, which is why she taught the formal methods in addition to the more intuitive elements of massage. Similarly, a lot of connecting to the sacred is about intuition, but sometimes it's nice to have one or more options. Sometimes these "fallback" options can become our primary method, and in turn, an integral aspect of who we are in this world.

The other potential advantage is that certain wise and accomplished beings have consecrated and blessed these images and imbued them with a spiritual power. So we get to borrow from their capacity. I've already spoken of this river of blessings, and it's kind of like that. It's also like joining a community of others, all rallying around this one image or being. There's something vitalizing about this for some of us.

It's really something to experience this idea of a communal river, oftentimes referred to as "lineage." I've had the experience of sitting in the company of high lamas who formally invoke their lineage of blessings through ceremonial ritual, and as if by magic or mass hypnosis, the deities that before were abstractions suddenly feel real to me, as real as any human being. Something has happened. It fades eventually (within hours, for an ordinary person like me), but I've touched it so I know what it feels like. Practice becomes a matter of learning to recalibrate my mind, heart, and being to be in alignment with the state I was in then.

When these lamas invoke these lineage of blessings, it's as if they're introducing us to their own tribe's intermediary. We shake hands with this new being, and from that point forward, it's up to us to uphold the vitality of that relationship or to let it slide. And this is also called *practice*.

I think it's very similar to how we can be with other human beings. Once you have a genuine connection to someone, even for a moment, you can then consciously choose to cultivate that relationship. It feels very similar with deities and spiritual/mythical beings. The only difference might be if you choose not to continue with the latter, they cease to feel real to you; it's as if they cease to exist, at least in our conscious awareness.

Revisiting Posture

Anthropologist Felicitas Goodman studied the relationship between mental states and ritual/ceremonial postures as depicted in statues across different cultures. She found that certain postures pointed to similar attitudes, mind-states, and meaning even across different cultures. [17]

When we hold our bodies a certain way, energy flows in a particular manner, giving rise to specific energetic, emotional, and mental states. Among the many postures that a human body can be held or contorted into, one in particular allows for a sense of reverence and connection to the divine that's universal. It's the posture of holding one's hands together in front of one's heart. This positioning of our hands in particular leads to our energy connecting and supporting a reverential state of mind and heart, which is why we take a similar posture when we take refuge or pray. We're working with energy. A lot of spiritual work is energy work in this way.

Taking such a posture is very different from placing one's hands on one's forehead, such as in other types of prayer. That creates a very different kind of energetic configuration. You might try taking this posture and noticing how the arms help to channel the energy from the ground to the head. *In my own experience, I've noticed that I tend to fall into this posture when I'm seeking answers to make decisions, as I'm bringing energy to the brain, in particular to the forehead or toward the frontal lobe.*

---

[17] See Belinda Gore's *Ecstatic Body Postures* for a summary of some of Goodman's work.

*But when we want to connect to the heart, we place
our hands in front of our hearts.* In this way, our
posture supports our intention, whether it's to connect to the heart or to think more clearly.

—Week four

My suggestions for practice this week are as follows:

Preliminary:

1. You've begun settling upon a *set* time and place.

2. Just as with last week, you take a relaxed and up-right posture in your seat and allow yourself to settle in.

Beginning:

3. Take refuge. See if you can make contact with some manifestation of the sacred for you, whether in the form of a deity, the beauty of the natural world, or even the openness of the moment. There are a wide variety of ways to do this, so I don't want to prescribe anything other than to remind you of the idea of seeking a form of blessing for your meditation endeavor.

I mentioned previously regarding bodhicitta, that *if* you contact the intention of bodhicitta through prayer, your prayer might sound like, "Help me to have greater awakeness, clarity, and openness so I can be of help to others." But how we bring refuge into the act is to simply invoke "God..." or "Lord Krishna..." or "Allah..." or whatever face of the divine that connects us from the heart prior to our prayer. We can think of this momentary contact with our particular visage or portal as the act of refuge.

4. Raise bodhicitta. Touch into some motivation that entails growth and has an impact upon others.

Middle:

5. I suggest you set your timer to **three minutes.** Start it after invoking bodhicitta. Then, practice.

6. When the timer goes off, try leafing through your notebook of notes (from weeks 2 and 3). Your eyes and mind might alight on just one passage, or you might read a few. The idea is for your mind to settle upon these ideas, to expose yourself to them repeatedly in the weeks, months, and years to come. Do this for as short as a minute, or as long as a three or four minutes.

Ending:

7. Quickly contemplate the value of what you've just done. (If you've forgotten, you might go back to the instructions for the "Ending" portion of your practice from week 3). Then, offer that value or merit for all beings.

As you might note, we're slowly putting together our container of practice. The beginning and end are now in place to support the growth of the middle, which is what the remainder of this book will address.

Chapter 10: The long journey

Back in the early 90's, I heard the saying, "the long-est journey in life is the journey from the head to the heart." I never truly liked the saying because it sounded froofy and New Agey, but it gave me a framework for thinking about some things. For example, in my late teens, I sometimes went to bookstores to read inspirational or spiritual books. While reading, I would feel genuinely inspired, and yet one or two hours later, I would end up back in my normal state, which was usually hating life or just wanting to eat a few bagels. I'd bemoan, "Why can't I hold onto that positive feeling or attitude I just had thirty minutes ago?" It was because the knowledge I gained while reading was all in my head and not yet in my heart. It hadn't gone very deeply into me so I wasn't living the ideas I was reading about.

Later, I heard a different way of describing it that made better sense to me. It's a description of how the brain has developed, from the amygdala out to the cortex to the neocortex. When we read a spiritual book or are processing complex information, the neocortex, or the newest part of the brain, is doing most of the work. But when we're stressed out, someone cuts us off in traffic, or hurls an insult our way, the instinctual side of our brain, the amygdala, is triggered. Some people call the amygdala the "reptilian" or "lizard" brain.

So I think of the neocortex as mapping to the "head" and the amygdala as mapping to the "heart," using the head-to-heart metaphor. This means that I can read a stack of spiritual books or go to a slew of inspiring talks and feel good about myself, but if the message is staying in the neocortex, it's not going to show up in my life when it really counts.

When I was about 20 or 21, I went to see a documentary movie about strip-mining on Native American soil and the tragic plight of the Native Americans. I cried for most of the movie. I was deeply moved and resolved, and came out of the movie thinking, "I'm going to move there (wherever it was in New Mexico) and fight for the Native American people's welfare." An hour later, I was wrapped up in myself again thinking about my grades, a girl, bagels, and so on, and I thought, "Forget it. There's nothing I can do to help." I had all these great feelings while watching the movie, but they didn't go very deep.

One of my teachers, Tsoknyi Rinpoche, says that practice is about sending a message from the neocortex down to the amygdala. Whether we're practicing with lovingkindness, compassion, renunciation, impermanence, or the illusory nature of reality, it's one thing for it to rest at the level of the neocortex. It's another for it to go deep into the instinctual centers of our brain.

The question then becomes, how do we do this?

The answer is simple—through repetition. We send the same message, over and over and over and over and over and over... until it gets down there and somehow burrows itself in, so it shows up when we most need it.

The Depth to which We're Trying to Transform

I first heard of the "Orange Juice Principle" from Wayne Dyer. It goes something like this: if you take an orange and squeeze it, what comes out? The answer is orange juice. If you give this orange to someone else and they squeeze it, what comes out? Again, orange juice. If you take this orange, stick it in a vice and squeeze it then, what comes out? Orange juice. And it goes on and on like this.

What's his point?

The point is that whatever is on the inside is what comes out. It doesn't matter who or what does the squeezing. So when life starts squeezing us, it's really not about who's doing the squeezing, why they're doing it, or why it's happening to us. And for a practitioner, it's not so much about the external circumstances of the situation. Instead, it's that what's on the inside is what comes out. The squeezing is simply an opportunity for us to see what we have on the inside. That's the productive use of the being-squeezed experience for a serious practitioner. If what's on the inside is grief—that is, we carry a lot of unresolved sadness from past losses—then when we're squeezed, we experience a lot of grief. If what's on the inside is anger, and we're squeezed, anger comes out. If what's on the inside is fear, and we're squeezed, fear comes out.

For example, when we feel very hungry, and we become irritable and angry, that tells us that we're carrying latent anger. There's no intrinsic need for anger as a response to hunger. Hunger is simply hunger. We can make up ailments or read books to solidify our supposed ailment. But from the perspective of the Orange Juice principle, it's quite simple. The hunger is simply the squeeze, and out comes anger. If we continually focus on avoiding hunger so as to avoid anger, we don't get at the simple truth that there's anger underneath, which keeps us from processing and working through the latent anger. I speak from my own experience on this particular issue. I used to become irritable when hungry until I began examining my own anger and working through it. For many years since, I've come to experience hunger as simply hunger, and not as trigger for anger or irritation.

I could tell the same story with tiredness. It's the squeeze. What comes out when tired is what's already inside.

If we reprogram our minds all the way down to the bottom with bodhicitta, or some other quality like that—and we're squeezed, then a variety of kindness naturally comes out. This is what we want as practitioners. It's one of our goals.

I once observed a stark instance of this orange juice principle in action. In the fall of 2001, I lived in the Washington DC area, not far from the Pentagon, which of course was one of the targets of the 9/11 attacks. When 9/11 happened, I saw that some people were very angry about the situation, some were very scared, and others were very sad. It was as if the recent events were squeezing out what was already on the inside. Those who had anger on the inside were now very angry at the turn of events. Those who held sadness within were now very sad, and those who had fear were now very scared. It was uncanny to me how predictable the reactions were just by what I already knew about the people.

Related to this, I've heard funerals described as socially-sanctioned events where grieving is allowed, especially for men. We live in a culture where men aren't encouraged to grieve, at least very openly. But funerals give social permission. It's as if the men say to themselves, "I can finally cry and wail." Who knows how much of the crying is about the actual loss of the person that the funeral is for, and how much of it is stored up grief from all the other past, ungrieved losses. The same can be said for relationship breakups. I often wonder how much of the grief is about the one person, and not the rest of one's life?

The point of practice then, is to transform what's at the bottom, at the level of the heart, to send a message from the head to the heart, from the neocortex to the amygdala.

I've attended talks and teachings of many kinds. I've read hundreds of books on various subjects, had incredible conversations with amazing people, journaled and thought about each of these encounters since then. My life has been enriched and informed by these things, but from the perspective of who I am when squeezed hard by life, when my instincts are severcly threatened, when I'm stressed to the gills— many of these things haven't done a whole lot for me, really.

What's made the difference in those difficult times is my practice, or the repetitive nature of my practice. That's what shows up in my consciousness when all is said and done. And today, most of what shows up during times of duress appears worthwhile to me. I'm convinced that what we call character is what's in our hearts, deep down in our being, and only practice, only repetition, only a conscious and repeated effort at transformation gets the message down there, if it isn't there already.

Pliable and Brittle

I've talked about shamatha, translated as "calm-abiding" or "pacifying" meditation. If you do it long enough, or even for a few minutes, you may notice that your mind is settled or not proliferating with as many thoughts, which allows it to abide more calmly in the moment. If you persist at this for a longer time, both longitudinally as well as per sitting, the thoughts settle even more, your energy relaxes further, and you enter a neutral state. Not positive nor negative, just neutral, or what some might call "calm."

One of my teachers likes to say that the point of practice isn't to become neutral, or even to have peace of mind. These instead are side effects and if all we're accomplishing in our practice is getting calm and neutral, then it's simply not enough to effect genuine transformation. So then why bother with shamatha?

As he puts it, the point of shamatha is to make the mind more *pliable*, or to increase its usability. What we think of as "calm and neutral," or even "centered," we can also think of as a mind that's more pliable, which I want to contrast with a mind that's *brittle*.

For example, if my mind is brittle and someone comes up to me and says, "Yuichi, you're an ugly guy" or something unpleasant like that, I'm likely going to get defensive and think or say something like, "How dare you!" I might even be tempted to strike back verbally. I might also take it personally and look in the mirror and think, "Oh my God, maybe he's right?"

So that's a brittle mind.

But if my mind is pliable, my reaction to the same comment might be, "Wow, I'm not sure why you would say that to me, but I'm sad to hear it. Then again, I can see you're upset, and you probably don't mean to hurt me." Having a pliable mind doesn't mean I don't feel an emotion in the moment, but I'm more present, not as reactive, and I can move with what's happening while focused just as much on the other as myself. So maybe "reactive" is a good synonym for "brittle?"

Suppose someone tells me, "Yuichi, shape up!" If my mind isn't pliable, the message won't go in deep, or at all. I may reject it outright simply because I don't like the tone. But with a pliable mind, my re-action might be closer to, "Wow, I don't like the tone of the message, but maybe there's some point to it? Maybe there's a way I can get in better shape and be more fit." And so with a pliable mind, I'm able to glean out the constructive element of someone else's advice despite the somewhat harsh tone of it. Con-trast this with what a brittle mind would do, which is likely to become defensive, if not reject the whole thing.

When we practice shamatha for even a few minutes, our minds become more open and pliable. But then, what do we do with our more pliable minds?

We begin re-moulding and re-programming it with certain kinds of information and ideas. The medita-tional method of reprogramming the head all the way to the heart—or the neocortex to the amygdala—is called contemplative or analytic meditation.

Contemplative/Analytic Meditation

The Dalai Lama was interviewed a few years ago and asked a question along the lines of, "Considering the myriad forms of meditation in the Tibetan tradition of Buddhism, what one meditation practice would you recommend to Westerners?" His answer: ana-lytic, or contemplative meditation.

Analytic meditation is an important and powerful form of meditation. For many Westerners, most of whom have an extensive educational background of at least a K-12 education, I think it will feel more natural than other forms of mediation, like shamatha, for example.

Catholicism has a practice very similar in spirit to contemplative meditation. It's called *lectio divina.* I've taken the following set of passages (unedited but truncated in places) from a website belonging to the Order of Carmelites (currently at ocarm.org/en) that describes the practice.

> **"Lectio Divina,"** a Latin term, means "divine reading" and describes a way of reading the Scriptures whereby we gradually let go of our own agenda and open ourselves to what God wants to say to us… the first stage is *lectio* (reading) where we read the Word of God, slowly and reflectively so that it sinks into us. Any passage of Scripture can be used for this way of prayer but the passage should not be too long.
>
> The second stage is *meditatio* (reflection) where we think about the text we have chosen and ruminate upon it so that we take from it what God wants to give us.
>
> The third stage is *oratio* (response) where we leave our thinking aside and simply let our hearts speak to God. This response is inspired by our reflection on the Word of God.

The final stage of Lectio Divina is *contemplatio* (rest) where we let go not only of our own ideas, plans and meditations but also of our holy words and thoughts. We simply rest in the Word of God. We listen at the deepest level of our being to God who speaks within us with a still small voice. As we listen, we are gradually transformed from within. Obviously this transformation will have a profound effect on the way we actually live and the way we live is the test of the authenticity of our prayer. We must take what we read in the Word of God into our daily lives.

The formulation within the Dharma is similar. But instead of (1) reading, (2) reflection, (3) response, and (4) rest, there is (1) listening, (2) reflecting, and (3) meditating (which includes resting the mind).

Because Buddhism has tended to be an oral tradition, it's said that one first has to hear the Dharma, thus, the **listening**. (In this day and age, many of us take notes in our notebooks at teachings, then use these notebooks as fodder for our contemplative practices.) Then, there's the cogitation and engagement of **reflection**, followed by an allowing of the ideas to go deeper within a more **meditative** state, with less of the cogitation as one rests the mind.

In actual practice, it might look something like this: suppose you went to a Dharma teaching where the teacher spoke of the importance of patience and its relationship to love, and summarized it using the line from the Corinthians, "love is patient." (Yes, we'll suppose that the Dharma teacher is being pluralistic in her religious approach!) You write it down in your notebook. Then during your own practice session, you might read it quietly a few times, and eventually repeat it in your mind a few more times, allowing each reading of it to sink a little deeper. The intent here is to allow for the mind to settle around the line.

You might then ask yourself, "What thoughts arise when I run this line through my mind? What does it mean to me?" You might think of times in your life when someone was patient with you, asking, "How did that feel? How is it different from when someone was impatient with me? What about when I'm being patient with someone else? How did that turn out? Or when I'm impatient? How is all this connected to love?"

If you're so inclined, you might even consider looking up the dictionary definitions of the various terms you come across, as well as the etymological origins, in order to gain deeper insight.

All this time, you're returning your mind to the line or verse itself as a kind of mental anchor, just as you would bring your mind back to your breath in shamatha. After reflecting in such a manner for a few minutes, exploring different connections and meanings around the verse, you'll want to sit with whatever state of being that's arisen, or with the sense of openness or connection that the reflections have brought about. You might even continue to occasionally repeat the phrase "love is patient" gently in your mind for when your mind wanders too far into cogitation.

This is a brief sampling of the practice of analytic meditation. You take a verse and begin *contemplating* around and about it. It's almost like "brainstorming," but with a stronger sense of an anchor around the verse. You can do this for a few minutes, alternating with a few minutes of resting the mind. Back-and-forth, but continually centered around the verse. This is how to slowly, through repetition, send the message (in this case, of the relevance of patience to love) from the neocortex down through the cortex, to the amygdala.

A key point to note in this practice is that the reflecting stage can be stimulating and interesting at first, but at some point, it can start to feel dull or even boring. It gets boring because it's repetitious. You may be able to reflect for 10 - 15 minutes the first day, another 10 - 15 minutes the next, but by the third or fourth day your mind will have exhausted all the possibilities—there's nothing new!—and you're bored with the same well-worn tracks of uninspired thoughts within the first five minutes!

This is when you want to continue to bring your mind back to the original verse at hand, repeatedly, not in a coerced, brute-force fashion, but gently, as in, "Let me simply sit with the verse and see if anything comes up. Even if the ideas are the same, let me sit with them so they might go deeper in me." The basic premise is that you're bringing your mind and your being to the verse, over and over, just as in shamatha you would bring your mind back to the breath again and again. This is the repetitive element.

It might not be true *for you*, but some readers might have an aversion to such repetitiveness in learning, not out of laziness, but more as an aversive reaction to rote learning. Here, I want briefly to introduce you to one of my favorite words, the verb "to conflate." Many of you will already be familiar, but to save some others the trouble of looking it up, I'll define it here. To conflate is *to combine two things or ideas (that are not necessarily the same) into one in one's mind*. For example, one could say, "Spirituality and religion tend to be conflated in some people's minds," which is to say that for some people, they are one and the same despite the fact that for many others, they are two distinct things.

So with regard to people's reactions to repetition, there is sometimes a conflating of **repetition** and **rote** learning in Western culture. A stark example of this occurs in mathematics teaching and learning. Some educators want to toss out repetitive elements of instruction for fear it will turn teaching into mindless, rote exercises. Others see the intrinsic value of repetition but don't *separate out* the mind-numbing aspects of rote, and so would urge for countless drill-and-kill exercises.

And yet, upon examination, repetition doesn't equate with rote. They are two distinct things. I've written a phenomenologically-tinged paper on this exact issue within mathematics education. [18] In the paper I argue that the primary distinction has to do with intent. There are repetitive acts that we engage in where the intent is toward mastery, learning, and growth, and as such, is accompanied by a certain level of mindful attentiveness. Examples might be how musicians or athletes perform countless repetitive acts during their training. In contrast, we can engage in repetitive acts without much care as to the consequence—such as mindlessly completing homework—and as such, it is done with very little mindful attention. When there is little intent toward mastery or learning, an activity easily deteriorates into rote, which has very little positive outcome.

---

[18] For those who are curious enough to labor through the short paper, it is entitled, "Teasing out Repetition from Rote: An Essay on Two Versions of Will" published in the journal, *Educational Studies in Mathematics*. It can be found on the internet, but also, you are welcome to write me for a copy at yhanda@gmail.com.

Repetition, as defined separately from rote, is necessary for deep and robust learning. It's the basis of any form of mastery, and it also happens to be the basis for contemplative meditation. Even the practice of shamatha is based upon repetition—that of bringing our awareness back to our breath, hundreds of thousands of times, across years of practice. But in all of these practices, the intent is learning and personal growth, so we're invested in the repetitive act, which is what gives it its power.

So when we approach a verse for contemplation and commit countless hours upon a line or two, even repeating some of the same thoughts around that line, we do so with an attitude of mindfulness. And in doing so, we imbue the repetitiveness with power. Just as one can take a hundred swings of a baseball, each with focused intent, one can run the same thought of "love is patient" through one's mind a hundred times, each with focused intent.

Perhaps you can imagine spending 15 minutes a day across a year contemplating that one line in the described manner. Something will likely have transformed within you at a profound level. Can you sense the difference in transformative power of that, in contrast to reading a few inspiring pages in a book, or even a few books on love and not returning to think upon it except on rare occasions? The former is proactive, whereas the latter is quite passive in its approach to personal transformation. This is the power of analytic meditation.

For this week, we'll focus on expanding the middle. I will abridge the items discussed at length previously.

Preliminary:
1. Set time and place.
2. Relaxed and upright posture; allow for some settling.

Beginning:
3. Refuge.
4. Bodhicitta.

Middle:
5. Timer set to **three minutes**, as was the case last week; practice shamatha for those three minutes.
6. Choose one passage. It can be a single line, but try to limit it to no more than three lines. It can come from a book, a talk, even a conversation. It can also be the line "love is patient." It should be

written down so your eyes can alight on it on a regular interval.

Spend a few minutes reflecting on its meaning to you, then relax into the state of being that this reflecting produces in you for a minute or two. This can take anywhere from one to five minutes total. For now, try to cap it at five minutes so you don't go longer than that for this week. Remember, we're aiming for long-term, continuous growth.

Ending:
7. Offer merit.

Chapter 11: Turning the mind toward practice

With the apparatus of analytic or contemplative meditation set up in our practice, the question now becomes, "What shall we set as the primary topic of contemplation?"

The purpose of this book is to help you to set up a daily meditation practice. To that end, I've discussed the notion of setting up a temporal container of practice, where we learn to say "no" to the many distractions that life poses, and instead, we practice. We learn to tell ourselves, "I acknowledge there are countless tasks that need attending to, but for now, I'm going to pause in the midst of all this activity, and I *will* practice."

One topic of contemplation is especially supportive of the intent to turn the mind toward practice. In fact, it's considered the single-most important subject of contemplation by many teachers of the

Dharma. It's not a stretch to say that all of the Buddha's teachings could be summarized in just this one topic; and that topic is impermanence.

> *Of all footprints, the elephant's are outstanding; just so, of all subjects of meditation for a follower of the Buddha, the idea of impermanence is unsurpassed.*[19]

When it comes to impermanence, we can examine it from a number of perspectives. For example, the chair or seat you've taken while reading is impermanent. It didn't always exist as it currently does, and in time, it will fall apart and lose its capacity as a chair, eventually turning to dust. There is also the kind of impermanence that involves your reputation, whether it is good or bad. It wasn't always the way it is now, and in time, it too will shift in one manner or another, if not disappear altogether in time. There's also the matter of your wealth or lack thereof, or even your karma. You can accumulate a lot of one or the other or both, and later, lose it all or burn through it in one form or another.

And yet, despite these myriad variations on contemplating impermanence, there is one form of it that

---

[19] Credit: Patrul Rinpoche, excerpts from *The Words of My Perfect Teacher*, translated by the Padmakara Translation Group. Copyright © 1994, 1998 by Padmakara Translation Group. Reprinted with the permission of The Permissions Company, Inc., on behalf of Shambhala Publications Inc., Boulder, Colorado, www.shambhala.com.

gets to the heart of the matter—and that's the contemplation of death, and specifically, of one's own death.

If you find yourself feeling uncomfortable with some of the ideas to come, please be aware of your discomfort. You shouldn't force yourself with these ideas. It may be that the timing isn't right for you. But if it's just a mild discomfort you feel, then it may help to become curious about what these ideas are triggering in you. Also, if you find yourself becoming deeply depressed over the contemplation of impermanence, please consider pulling back from it. Contemplating impermanence and death serves no purpose if it causes you to become depressed and paralyzed in your life. It's considered part of skillful means—i.e. relative bodhicitta—on my part as your guide, but also *on your part for yourself,* to discern when a particular method is helping you to open up and to move toward meaningful transformation, and when it is not.

If heavy depression turns out to be your reaction, it may be that receiving help from qualified professionals along with more slowly building a modest practice, will benefit you in the long run. If that is the case, you might simply skim the rest of the book while setting a long-term plan of developing your practice until you've reached twenty or thirty minutes a day. You might add two minutes to your total practice every two weeks until you've reached your desired goal.

A helpful alternative to contemplating impermanence is to practice any form of lovingkindness meditation, or simply contemplating verses focused on loving-kindness (*metta* or *maitri*), particularly toward yourself. There are many excellent books on this topic.[20] Once you establish a more stable practice, along with lovingkindness toward yourself, you might consider returning to the contemplations that follow.

We live in a culture where talking about death is uncomfortable. To turn the mind, suddenly, toward such a taboo topic can be jarring to the mind. Please be aware and try not to run roughshod over your inner reactions to what follows. Instead, I encourage you to be sensitive to your own reactions while also trying to maintain an open mind.

The remainder of this book will be centered around a verse taken from Patrul Rinpoche's classic book, *Words of My Perfect Teacher: A Complete Translation of a Classic Introduction to Tibetan Buddhism.* I've chosen this particular verse because it's one that summarizes well the many facets of impermanence, but also, if the reader finds something of value here and is not familiar with his book, perhaps the reader will feel inspired to continue on to the

---

[20] In particular, you might consider reading any of Pema Chodron's books, or else Sharon Salzberg's *Lovingkindness: The Revolutionary Art of Happiness.*

vastly superior and more deeply inspired book from this one.

The verse, in its entirety, is this:

> *Whatever is born is impermanent and is*
> *bound to die.*
> *Whatever is stored up is impermanent and is*
> *bound to run out.*
> *Whatever comes together is impermanent and*
> *is bound to come apart.*
> *Whatever is built is impermanent and is*
> *bound to collapse.*
> *Whatever rises up is impermanent and is*
> *bound to fall down.*
> *So also, friendship and enmity, fortune and*
> *sorrow, good and evil,*
> *all the thoughts that run through one's*
> *mind—everything is always changing.*[21]

For this chapter, along with the next two, I will focus only on the first line: *Whatever is born is impermanent and is bound to die.*

You might note that it's a very matter-of-fact statement, rather inarguable and clearly not an imputation

---

[21] Credit: Patrul Rinpoche, excerpts from *The Words of My Perfect Teacher*, translated by the Padmakara Translation Group. Copyright © 1994, 1998 by Padmakara Translation Group. Reprinted with the permission of The Permissions Company, Inc., on behalf of Shambhala Publications Inc., Boulder, Colorado, www.shambhala.com.

upon reality. That is, we're not wishing or hoping that something is or isn't so. We're not pasting a positive or negative slant upon the nature of reality. The statement is purely descriptive of things as they are.

I'd now like to suggest a short exercise using this line (*"Whatever is born is impermanent and is bound to die"*). Have the line written somewhere in front of you, or leave this page open in front of you as you attend to this exercise. You might find that if you can cognitively offload the line onto the paper or computer screen, it will allow your mind to move more freely *around* the line itself.

Exercise: Sit quietly for a few minutes as you reflect upon this line and see what comes up for you. For example, maybe what comes up is anger, as in "I don't want to be thinking about this." Or sadness, as in "This is so depressing. What's the point?!" Or maybe it's a sense of relief. My suggestion is not to stifle such thoughts and emotions, but simply to notice them. You might even jot down any insights that occur to you during the exercise.

[Pause in reading to engage in a few minutes of contemplation]

The following reactions are not uncommon:
- A desire for wanting to appreciate and to be present in each moment since "whatever is

born" can be a friendship, a situation, a life, or anything, and it all changes.

- A numbness to the notion of death; not being able to penetrate its reality, or it not penetrating the mind.
- An urge to love those around us more deeply, even asking ourselves, "Am I loving everything and everyone enough?"
- Sadness about others who may die, or fear around our own death.
- A desire to begin identifying with the aspect of ourselves that might survive death, and to live from that place more often.
- A sense of relief, not so much that one will eventually escape through death, but through a larger perspective that allows us to see that a lot of the things we normally stress ourselves out over don't matter so much.
- A surge of joy, simply that nothing is permanent, that we're here, we do our thing, and then it's all gone. And that we're all in it together!
- A sense of everything dissolving and merging with the rest; not so personal in nature, but almost impersonal.
- A sudden sense that we're wasting time on things that don't matter.

The contemplation of death is considered to be at the heart of contemplating impermanence. And within the contemplation of death, it's the contemplation of *our own* death that's considered the core practice. So we contemplate our own death.

And why do we do this?

Many of us become wrapped up in a world of inanities, trivialities, and distractions, and we lose sight of our deepest priorities. If we examine how we're living our lives from the perspective of our own death, it's not so hard to see how most of us waste a lot of time on things that don't matter, and in turn, we're more likely to begin appreciating what's in front of us in the present moment. Simply put, the contemplation of our own death helps us live more deeply in the present moment while attending to our most heartfelt priorities.

If you happen to be out of high school, you might know the experience of looking back upon your high school years and realizing how much time and energy you spent worrying about things that seem entirely trivial to the current you. You might also think back upon how much more you could have appreciated what you had. If you're past your 20's, you could probably say the same about your 20's. And same with your 30's, and so on.

Contemplating your own death enables you to take the furthest perspective from within this lifetime. It's not that different from a high school student imagining his current life from the perspective of his 30-year-old self. The more realistic and tangible his contemplation, the more easily he can relinquish many of his worries, and in turn, begin opening up to the joys, beauty, love, and even the miraculous around him in the present. This is one of the ways in which contemplating our own death can profoundly affect how we live in the present.

But also, contemplating our death can help us to see just how unpredictable death is. The fact is, our lives can end at any point. Any one of us could unexpectedly suffer a stroke in the middle of the night, or get run over on the way home, or grow multiple tumors in our brains in the next month. There's no sense of when we're going to die or how it's going to happen. Someone could gun us down tomorrow, or we could live for twenty-five more years and fall from a cliff. There's no guarantee, and there's no protection against this. Death can come anytime, in any form.

And yet many of us live as if we have a long time ahead. If you're 30, you might think in the back of your mind that you have another 50 plus years to live. Many of my 20-year-old university students act as if death were a theoretical concept, and not a reality for most of them.

When we regularly contemplate the fact that we could die tomorrow, or next week, or God knows when, we slowly and *subtly* begin changing the way we live. Sometimes the changes are drastic and dramatic, such as quitting a job or ending a relationship,

but for the most part, the shifts are gradual and cu-
mulative, and the product of regular and *repeated*
practice. As we think about our own death and its
unpredictability, the more inclined we are to turn our
minds toward something larger or more profound
than the usual thoughts of making more money, finding a better career, getting a date or a divorce, and
even more mundane issues like becoming emotional
over facebook posts, eating organic or not, sushi or
salad, black dress or blue pants, and so on and so
forth. We're less inclined to get bent out of shape
over such inanities.

As we slowly shed our concerns with what we begin
to see as trivialities, we start to turn our minds toward deeper concerns. As this process unfolds, we
find that the core of our concerns is spiritual, and in
particular, that of deepening our spiritual condi-
tion. In this way, the contemplation of impermanence is said to light a fire in us to practice.

From the perspective of our own death, priorities
begin to realign, and if we have it in us to practice toward a deeper happiness (i.e., enlightenment), the
impulse toward that deeper fulfillment begins assert-
ing itself more strongly in how we live.

I spent close to a year utilizing 20 - 30 minutes of my
daily practice time contemplating death, mostly my
own. By the end of that year, my relationship to my
own practice felt vastly different. I had already been
meditating for close to 20 years at that point, and yet,

deep down I held a somewhat resistant attitude toward practice, as if it were some kind of chore. But by about the three-month point of contemplating death and impermanence, I stopped looking at practice as a chore or as a spiritual obligation. Instead, my attitude became more of, "Why wouldn't I spend more time at this?" The importance of many other pursuits (that ultimately weren't fulfilling to a deeper part of me) seemed to fade, which opened up more time and gave me more energy toward practice and all that it entailed.

Whereas sitting for an hour a day seemed like a pretty big deal, it suddenly *felt* like nothing. Now, staying on my cushion for an hour or two at a time seemed like no big deal. It was more of a delight, and again, I often couldn't imagine anything else more meaningful or satisfying, both in terms of my actual experience as well as from a philosophical perspective.

In this way, the more we contemplate impermanence and death, the less likely we are to grasp at things in this world. This *is* spiritual technology at its finest. You fill your mind with thoughts of impermanence and death, and the mind eventually relaxes from its regular clinging. In short, it relaxes.

Many of us *grasp* for things in life, such as "I want a job. I want money. I want an identity as having a career. I want a partner so I can hold onto them. I want to create children, and I want to have friends." *We don't simply desire them. We cling to these desires.* And yet, if we truly hear the message of impermanence *in our hearts, in our amygdala, down to our core,* the clinging slowly abates.

This doesn't mean that we become a hermit or a recluse and retreat from life. It also doesn't mean we don't pursue our goals and dreams in this life. It just means we do it with less clinging (or clingy) intent and energy. We lessen our attachments to whatever degree that the understanding of impermanence has permeated our being. Even the slightest lessening of our clinging makes a world of difference in how we go about our pursuits and endeavors.

Suppose you have the belief that says that you need friends to be happy. That's a belief. And suppose you cling to that belief. You might find articles on the internet that support your belief, some of which might even be backed up by science (or to be more rigorous about it, the soft sciences, such as psychology and sociology). Maybe you begin sharing your belief with others, and as you get positive feedback (and very little resistance), the intensity of your belief grows—that is, your attachment to the belief grows. Then you meet someone who you think is a potential best friend. What happens? Most likely, you start clinging. There's a kind of desperation beneath your interactions. If not a friendship, then the same can be said for romantic relationships, for many.

But there's another way. Imagine that there isn't an
attachment to the belief and instead, you think, "It
would be nice to have some friends, but if not, that's
good too." This is a more relaxed attitude. It allows
for people and things to come and go without you
losing your peace. If you meet someone, you might
simply have a nice time, try to be kind and
open. This is a vastly different kind of energy and
approach to friendship. It's also more likely that
you'll form relaxed friendships based upon trust,
without the clinging.

The contemplation of impermanence and death helps
us to release our various manners of clinging,
whether to people and things or to our inner thoughts
and belief systems. The more we contemplate impermanence, both the gross and subtle forms of clinging
ease up. Ultimately, the contemplation of impermanence and death addresses our various attachments,
both inner and outer.

In the four noble truths, the Buddha taught that the
cause of suffering is our clinging and attachment. So
the contemplation of impermanence helps alleviate
our suffering since it reduces attachment. As far as
our own practice is concerned, as we slowly release
our clinging, we become more inclined to practice
because we aren't so wrapped up in the countless
tasks and pursuits of ordinary living. We're less
busy in mind and body. We still live our ordinary
lives, but we're not swung around by it, emotionally
and mentally, to the same extent. We can see

through it: "This isn't very important. That isn't so important either in the great scheme of things. It's just a fact of life and I have to deal with it. It is what it is. There are more important things in life to concern myself with." In this way, we learn to relax and are able to practice more deeply, while also dealing with the facts of life with greater equanimity and peace.

When I first envisioned this book, the practice of contemplating impermanence is what I held to be the central piece that would ignite a fervor for practice. *Personally, I can't think of anything more valuable and powerful in trying to establish a daily meditation practice than the contemplation of impermanence and death.*

To give a sense for how I engage in such contemplation, I'll briefly share how I might begin. What follows in italics, is a sample interior monologue (a rather cleaned up and coherent version):

There are two things that I know about death. One is that I don't know <u>when</u> it's going to happen, and two is that I don't know <u>how</u> it's going to happen. So, it can happen tomorrow, a month from now, a year from now, thirty years from now... I just don't know. I also don't know how it's going to be happen. It might be extremely painful. It could be humiliating, such as through the loss of bodily functions. Or it could be a very peaceful kind of death, such as in my sleep. I have no idea.

And sometimes, I go through every scenario that occurs to me.

Maybe my death will happen while driving. Maybe I will get hit by a car while riding my bike. Or maybe I will be shot. Or it could be cancer, or some infection. A stroke. Death in a fire or drowning. I just don't know.

And then I consider what happens to me afterwards.

I haven't a clue. Different religions tell me different stories. Atheists tell their own story of an abrupt ending, but no one seems to know for sure. So, I have no deep conviction of what will truly happen. My personal belief is that whoever I identify with as myself right now will surely cease while something else continues. Many spiritual traditions speak of something continuing. I wouldn't have a clue what that is. I can choose to believe it—and practice a kind of faith—but in all honesty, I don't <u>know</u> the truth of it.

And again, the time of death is uncertain. So, the person I know as Yuichi could perish later today for all I know.

I also reflect on the deaths of those around me.

What of my friends? They will die also. My parents (who are still alive) will also pass away and disappear from my life. Even the middle-school students I see every day on my way to work will die. And they're all younger than me. And their children will die. All the babies in carriages will someday pass away as well.

Whenever I think of people younger than me dying, the reality of death has a much more powerful impact. It somehow wakes me up out of my dream of things going according to some unconscious expectation.

Every animal I see will die. And every insect I see or can't see will die. Every being that's currently alive on this planet will face death and will perish.

These are the kinds of thoughts I run through my mind based on the original line, *"Whatever is born is impermanent and is bound to die."* I sometimes imagine that this one line is the basic melody in a jazz standard, and I'm riffing off of it. I'm running variations of that thought, improvising new and related thoughts, but continually centered around the original line. If I get lost or too far off, I'll come back to it by reciting it a few times, and then listen carefully for what it brings up anew.

Working with Sadness

Sometimes I focus on the eventual death of someone very close, someone whose death I would mourn deeply. As I think of that person's death, it can bring up tremendous sadness. As the sadness arises, I stay with it, letting it be within me. When I feel this kind of emotion during contemplation of death, I often note how the sadness points me toward some buried attachment I'm carrying. It's not that the sadness *is* attachment, but more often than not, within the sadness is a mix of "clean" and "dirty" emotions, or pain.[22] The "clean" side of it is the plain sadness, while the "dirty" side of it is a heavy, attached quality of clinging, usually deriving from some belief that's out of sync with the nature of reality. When I sit with the sadness, it's not that I'm trying to loosen myself of the "clean" and natural kind of sadness, but more the clinging quality and corresponding false beliefs.

With the clinging, I usually haven't *fully* let go to the fact that this person is mortal and that he or she could disappear from my life at any point. Or vice versa. Both would be beyond my control. Also, I occasionally tend to have an unhealthy sense of self-blame or over-responsibility buried, that comes to the fore as I sit with the feelings.

So as I think about this person's eventual death, this mixed quality of sadness often arises. I don't then say to myself, "Yuichi, you're a bad practitioner" or

---

[22] Taken from Acceptance and Commitment Therapy ("ACT").

"Yuichi, you shouldn't cling so much." Instead, I think, "I have some sadness, and I'm also attached here. I can allow myself to be that way for now and feel how that is, as it is," and that's exactly what I do. I peel off of the cognitive aspects of the contemplation for a few moments and allow myself to touch into the mixed bag of sadness that's arisen, and allow the feelings to be, without trying to overcome or get rid of them.

I imagine this "allowing" to be like a purifying process, as if by bringing my awareness to these feelings, the clinging can loosen from the sadness and slowly burn away. At the very least, by sitting with this mixed bag of feelings, I become more familiar with them, and with familiarity, I'm able to tease out the constituent elements of it in time. As I see more clearly what constitutes this experience that I call sadness-clinging, I can begin to let go of that which clings and inhibits, while honoring that which simply calls for feeling and inhabiting.

Sometimes, the feelings that arise stay for a while and fade, and other times, they feel overwhelmingly strong. If the latter, I sit with them for however long I can. When it gets to be a bit much, I move on, knowing that I'll come back to it the next day and the days following, if need be. As the proverb on how to eat an elephant goes, it's "one bite at a time."

The next day using the same contemplation, I might still feel the same mixed feelings of sadness. And the day after. But as I continue to touch into the sadness, I find that I'm able to loosen the underlying clinging.

My ex-wife, Bang, who has become one of my closest friends—or a kind of spiritual sister—is one such person whose death I've contemplated. She has suffered from lupus for at least the past 25 years of her life. Her kidneys failed about six years ago, and she has been on dialysis ever since. Every time she gets a simple cold or an infection, it's a life-or-death matter. And so, the thought of her suffering used to bring up a sense of internal panic and grief for me.

When I began contemplating her death, I felt tremendous and *overwhelming* sadness and attachment. I would simply recite the thought, "One day, Bang will pass away," and that thought would act as a dredger of intense attachment that I held to her—not just for her presence in my life, but for her feeling healthy and happy. And yes, it was deep-seated attachment I held for her. As wonderful as it may sound to care for someone to such a degree, it turned out to serve little purpose for her, or for me, as I will explain.

My acute attachment to her well-being and to her staying alive was almost a refusal on my part to allow her to suffer or die (as if I had any control over it). If I could have vocalized my basic attitude toward her, it probably would have sounded like, "You *cannot* die! You have to stay alive on my behalf!" And "You also have to be well so I don't have to worry so much!" But in time, through this one practice, a lot of this self-preoccupied attachment loosened. It got to the point where I had some semblance of peace and balance—some equanimity. I simply had more acceptance about it. I still feel heart-felt sadness, and sometimes even spontaneously break down in tears while talking with her, but the attached quality feels significantly loosened. In fact, I'm convinced that the loosening of the clinging is what allows me simply to cry, sometimes, seemingly "without reason."

It turns out this has had a not-so-subtle effect on my current relationship with her. I bring much less of my baggage into our relationship, particularly when she's suffering from her illness. Before, I sometimes would feel overwhelmed and think, "I can't deal with this. It's too much!" And I would become upset at myself and the situation due to my unresolved clinging. Today, I'm more often able to think, "I'll just be here with you. I can just listen, and I'll suffer alongside of you because that's part of my happiness." In this way, processing the initial sadness and clinging has helped me to become more present to her while she's alive, and for that, I am profoundly grateful.

If sadness is also a common emotion for you when contemplating the topic of death, I urge you to learn to befriend the experience, and begin to discriminate between that which is "clean" and that which is "dirty," or "clinging" in nature. The former is likely inevitable and even necessary while the latter, often

held up by our false beliefs, can come to be seen as
optional and even unhelpful for ourselves and others.

—Week six

For this week, we'll continue to focus on expanding the middle. I've abridged those items that were previously discussed at length.

Preliminary:
1. Set time and place.
2. Relaxed and upright posture; allow for some settling.

Beginning:
3. Refuge.
4. Bodhicitta.

Middle:
5. Timer set to **three minutes**, as was the case last week, and practice shamatha for those three minutes.
6. Re-set the timer to **five minutes,** take the line "*Whatever is born is impermanent and is bound to die*" and use it as the basis for contemplation. You might just sit with that line and see what comes up for you, or you can think through

its meaning and repercussions, as I illustrated earlier in this chapter. Or you can do some combination of both.

Toward the end of the time, relax into the state of being that the reflecting produces in you. Aim for about **eight total minutes of practice time.**

Ending:
7. Offer merit.

Chapter 12:
Contemplating death

The true aim in contemplating impermanence and death is to create a fire or yearning inside of oneself toward practice, the Dharma, or the spiritual. It's this fire that compels one back to one's practice, again and again. Without it, a sustainable, consistent practice is unlikely.

Initially or for a while, meditation *feels* nice for most of us. We see more clearly, we're calmer, and so on. But there will come a point when things *don't* feel better, or we may even feel worse. The question is, do we show up and practice anyway? I believe when it gets to this point, unless a genuine yearning or fire exists inside us, or even a glimmer of one, the practice *will* fall apart.

The contemplation of impermanence is meant to ignite and sustain that fire. It's one of the four thoughts that turn the mind toward the Dharma, as practiced in the Tibetan Buddhist tradition. [23]

Once we have a practice, we can engage in other practices within that container. We can further develop bodhicitta. We can learn tantra, which concerns itself with transforming our afflictive emotions into something beneficial. We can learn new technologies of the mind and heart, but these technologies require a container of some kind, a *practice*.

It's said that to be a dedicated practitioner, one has to move toward the Dharma as someone with their hair on fire runs to water. With that sense of urgency, enlightenment is not far off. Maybe this is an extreme version of it than what most of us want. Minimally, we want a small fire in our hearts, one that would sustain a daily practice of some kind.

Another way to describe this fire, and the word that's often used, is "renunciation." It doesn't mean that we become hermits and shun the world, but rather we

---

[23] The four thoughts are (1) the contemplation of this precious human birth, (2) the contemplation of impermanence, (3) the contemplation of the dissatisfaction of *samsara*, and (4) the contemplation of karma. I recommend Khandro Rinpoche's *This Precious Life* for an elaboration of the four thoughts. I chose to focus strictly on the second of the four contemplations for this book, as I consider it the heart of the four thoughts and that which ties them altogether.

become weary of the repeated disappointments resulting from seeking lasting fulfillment in worldly, or *samsaric* pursuits. This weariness propels our renunciation, that as we nurture it within ourselves, our motivation to put an end to suffering grows. This increased motivation to end our suffering *is* the heart of renunciation.

Renunciation can also be thought of as leading to a capacity for living in the world without being of it, similar to the notion of learning to wear the world like a loose garment. It's about partaking in the world, while being able to cast it off at any given moment. Or as the Zen teacher, Aitken Roshi, puts it, "Renunciation isn't giving things up. It's fully accepting that they pass away." We can still have desires and preferences, and yet, even when these aren't fulfilled, we're still at peace.

In the Theravada Buddhist tradition, monks and nuns often recite the "five remembrances":

> *I am subject to aging, have not gone beyond*
> *aging. This is the first fact that one should*
> *reflect on often, whether one is a woman or a*
> *man, lay or ordained.*
> *I am subject to illness, have not gone beyond*
> *illness...*
> *I am subject to death, have not gone beyond*
> *death...*
> *I will grow different, separate from all that is*
> *dear and appealing to me...*

> *I am the owner of my actions, heir to my actions, born of my actions, related through my actions, and have my actions as my arbitrator. Whatever I do, for good or for evil, to that I will fall heir...*

As you read these lines, it might be a worthwhile exercise to notice if any resistance arises in you. For example, sometimes I have a resistance to the second line, on illness. I don't want to think that, but the fact is, this body grows old and dies, and along the way encounters illness many times over.

Sometimes the fourth line brings up attachment mixed with sadness for me, which tells me I'm still clinging in some ways. So I can keep getting in touch with how I cling, and eventually I relax. This doesn't mean I become a cold human being, but rather, I accept the changing nature of my relationships. In turn, I can cherish and love people even more preciously knowing that I can't hold onto them forever.

The last line refers to karma. What we "fall heir to" is our habits of mind, our tendencies. If our tendency is to be kind to people, that's what we take with us into our future. If our tendency is to be consumed with greed, then that's the habit that will carry over. All we're carrying over is our karma, according to Buddhist belief. Rather than thinking in terms of reincarnation, we can also think of this on a day-to-day basis as well. Each night when we go to bed is a kind of death. And in the morning, we're incarnating into a new life, a new self, so to speak. When we go to sleep, we don't take any of the people we love; we just slink into our sleep by ourselves. And we wake up with the remnant of the patterns of mind and emotions we carried into our sleep. So if we go to bed angry, we might wake up hung over emotionally.

Exercise

Here is a very simple exercise. Whatever time it is right now, add 24 hours to it, and imagine that that's your time of death. In other words, this is a fantasizing exercise where you imagine that you only have 24 hours to live.

First, settle your mind for a minute or two, and then conjure this idea of your impending death so it feels as real as possible. As you hold this thought, notice what arises. What comes up for you when you know you have only 24 hours to live?

You may want to stay with this for a few minutes and afterwards, jot down what arose for you.

Perhaps you wanted to reach out to everyone you loved to let them know how much you appreciated their presence in your life? Or maybe you were worried about leaving your child without a parent? Or maybe you thought of all the things you would choose not to do, such as going to work or worrying about your finances, as you usually might?

This exercise *is* a practice in itself. It's a practice that one can do daily or a few times a week for just a few minutes. I find that this exercise tells me where I am in my life. It reveals to me how aligned I am with my deepest aspirations. I've used it to re-align myself, as well as gain greater insight into where I'm living with more integrity than in other places. When I persist at this, I'm consistently brought back to my practice because practice *is* the way back to truer alignment and deeper integrity.

At the same time, I want to point out what may be an obvious fact—that we need not impulsively act on what arises. For example, a common thing that comes up for many is that they wouldn't go to work if they had only 24 hours left to live. This doesn't mean then, that everyone should skip work each time they do this meditation. Instead, I think this exercise is better utilized as a gauge for where one's true priorities are, where one's heart's desires rest. For example, if I do this exercise every day for a month, and my answer is continually, "I wouldn't go to work," I might want to begin examining my relationship to work with questions such as, "Is this the work I want to be doing?" Or "Is there something at work I can change so it doesn't keep coming up like this?" Or "Can I change my attitude in relation to work, or else, can I find a way to cut back in my relationship to work that would appease whatever dissatisfaction I'm clearly experiencing?"

Or when family members come up in mind, maybe it speaks to some part of us that wants to be closer to family. Maybe we aren't honoring those relationships enough?

Again, a literal interpretation isn't the way to work with this exercise, but rather *hearing* what's truly important. One could even journal afterwards.

If what comes up for you is how profoundly sad you feel at how unprepared your own child would be for your untimely death, this isn't a sign that you necessarily need to sit down with your child and tell them, "Everything is impermanent. I could die anytime. That's what the Buddha said." Instead, you might ask yourself questions such as, "Why do I believe my child would be unprepared for my death?" or "What are the traits I would like my child to have so they could survive and potentially even thrive upon my death?" These may lead to questions such as, "Am I living as an embodiment of these same qualities in my own life so I can be a model for my child?" or "Am I bringing into my own life people who embody these qualities so my child will continue to have similar models beyond my own potential untimely death?"

I would like to share a personal story related to this.

When I was 12, my father quit his corporate job in Japan to begin a new business in the United States. As a consequence, we lived lean, financially, for a few years. Even though my parents never spoke of their financial insecurity, it was during this time that I began experiencing my own feelings of financial lack that would persist for the next few decades.

Looking back, what strikes me most prominently is that I was like a sponge to my parent's unspoken thoughts, to their energetic being. They very likely carried deep financial anxieties at the time, which they lovingly tried to protect me from. And yet, it's not what they said, but what they felt and embodied that, I believe, transferred into me.

I think sometimes we overlook the fact that the deepest and most lasting messages we offer to children (as well as others) has to do with our *being*. Not what we say or do, but the energy we carry in our personhood. If we're living a life that is profoundly open-hearted and courageous as parents, we transmit that exact quality of being to our children. On the other hand, if we're living a life scurrying for money, filled with unresolved financial anxieties and worried about this and that, I imagine these are the traits we're transmitting toward our children. If viewed through this lens, our concerns for our own children can be utilized as a springboard for living a life that's more deeply aligned with our deepest values.

The possibilities for insight and further action are limitless insofar as how this exercise can inform how we live.

And yet, it's been my own experience that as I slowly begin realigning my life with the various questions and insights that arise through this practice—that is, as I'm "straightening things out" here—it opens up space within me to move more closely toward the transcendent, toward the Dharma, toward practice. It's as if I've made deeper peace with much of the daily, worldly aspects of my existence. The people in my life come to know that I love them, and further communication on that matter doesn't seem quite as important, and in turn, resting in spirit, so as to prepare myself for the impending transition seems paramount. This is nothing other than practice. And of course, if I don't die immediately, it's no disappointment, as my practice allows me to live from a deeper and more open place within my own being, leading to a much more contented and joy-filled life.

In short, the contemplation of death—whether our own or that of others—is one of the greatest supports we can find for our daily lives, as well as for our daily meditation practice.

For this week, we'll continue focusing on expanding the middle.

Preliminary:
1. Set time and place.
2. Relaxed and upright posture; allow for some set-tling.

Beginning:
3. Refuge.
4. Bodhicitta.

Middle:
5. Set timer to **four minutes** and practice shamatha for those four minutes.
6. Re-set the timer to **six minutes,** and engage in one of the following two contemplative exercises, or some combination:

   a. Take the line *"Whatever is born is imper-manent and is bound to die"* and use that as the basis for contemplation.

b. Repeat the "24 hours to live" exercise from this chapter. You might even jot down some of the thoughts and feelings that surface for you.

Toward the end of the time, relax into the state of being that the reflecting produces in you. We're aiming for about **ten total minutes of practice time.**

Ending:
7. Offer merit.

Chapter 13: Continuing to contemplate death

I'd like to suggest a simple exercise to start off the chapter. Look at yourself in the mirror under normal lighting conditions and notice what arises in your mind and in your heart. This isn't about doing affirmations to make yourself feel better. There shouldn't be any censoring or vetting of your own thoughts and feelings. Simply look. No agenda. Or at least no conscious agenda other than noticing what arises within you.

To help with this exercise, you might take on an attitude of a "meditative state" or even an "experimental state." Try to be detached about what you notice going on in your mind and heart. See what shows up in your thoughts and emotions, as if you were doing an experiment tracking your reactions to seeing your own reflection.

Do self-critical thoughts come up? Self-flattery? Or do you find yourself tilting your head so as to reveal to you your better side? Or the opposite? Or are your thoughts more objective in nature without a lot of emotional charge, as if you were commenting on a stranger's face?

Go ahead and try it!

Regardless of the quality of thoughts, were you able to be objective *in your relation* to them? It's entirely possible to have strongly-charged self-critical thoughts that you simply notice yourself having. In other words, there's no inherent problem in having highly self-critical thoughts. It's our reaction to these thoughts that we want to be aware of. This *is* mindfulness in action.

When I was younger, I used to do this exercise as a way of seeing into my own self-image, or how I perceived myself. I would stand in front of a mirror for about three to five minutes. After an initial barrage of self-judgments and semi-conscious attempts to "look for the good," these emotionally-laden thoughts and gestures would pass, and I would begin to see past the usual layers of positive and negative judgments and opinions about my appearance. I found it liberating, simply seeing myself—at least the physical representation of my face—without the filters of opinions directed at the self.

Something very similar can be done with one's own speaking voice. When I first began teaching, I was interested in strengthening my voice and improving my articulation to become a better speaker. I read a number of books on the topic, and the most helpful suggestion was simply to record myself while teaching or having a conversation, and to listen to it afterwards.

Similar to the mirror exercise, the idea was simply to listen, and in particular, *to make no conscious attempt at changing one's speaking habits upon listening to how one sounds.* For example, when I did the exercise, if I caught myself frequently saying, "you know," I didn't then try to eliminate it from my speech pattern. Instead, I simply listened to the recording and was present to the experience of hearing myself, which was mostly experiencing the phenomenon of cringing at first. And yet, when I decided simply to listen and allow for the judgmental, evaluative thoughts to arise without wishing they weren't there, eventually they began to subside. Fairly quickly I was able just to hear myself speak. I heard my speech patterns, the tonality of my voice, the rhythm of my speech, and so on. I also noted where I felt uncomfortable listening and where I didn't. If I was conscious of anything, it was that I was going along with the primary suggestion of that author—*to restrain my tendency to want to fix anything in my speaking voice.*

At a later point, when I said "you know" while talking or teaching, I clearly heard it. I realized that until that point, I had never truly heard myself saying "you know" in action. Now that I heard it, it became natural not to use it, so it naturally fell away from my speaking habits. This felt vastly different from an alternative approach of making a concerted effort and commitment to eradicating it from my speech, and being on guard to make sure I never did it again. There would have been something forceful and aggressive about this latter approach.

The former approach felt *self*-correcting, almost effortless, and at the same time, it was effective. I hadn't made a conscious effort to change anything, it just sort of fixed itself, more or less, but with awareness. All that it took was for me to *restrain* my impulses at conscious correction until I could truly hear myself speak. Not that conscious change is bad in itself, except when it's motivated by emotionally-charged self-judgment and self-aggression, which oftentimes involves a sense of shame or non-acceptance. This is vastly different from a motivation say for clearer communication, which I've found is a more sustaining motivation.

I came across this same idea when I took a series of workshops in the Alexander Technique, which concerns itself with the various tensions we hold in our body that oftentimes result in poor body awareness and posture. On the first day of the workshop, the facilitator instructed, "Become aware of your posture," at which point many of us in the workshop straightened up in our seats.

But she had only told us to *become aware* of our posture. Not to fix it.

The facilitator went on to explain that when we make a conscious effort at fixing something *before* we bring full awareness to it, the change is consistently short-term. It's only good for as long as we're consciously aware of the thing we're trying to fix. As soon as our minds are off of it, we revert to our habitual patterns, in this case, of poor posture.

So when she said, "Become aware of your posture," she literally meant to be aware and not to straighten anything out. Be aware of how it felt, if and where there was tension, constriction, openness, and so on.

She referred to the principle in the Alexander Technique called "inhibition," which in this instance had to do with *inhibiting* an unconscious tendency or impulse to fixing our posture as a knee-jerk reaction, and in so doing, *allowing for awareness to enter instead.* With the entering of awareness, other non-habitual options avail themselves, including specific principles that allow for the body to relax and in turn rise up to its natural, upright posture of its own accord.

This same idea, across all three of the previous examples—seeing one's reflection in a mirror, hearing one's own voice in a recording, and working with one's posture—points to a basic principle in meditation. It's the same when we work with our emotions, such as with anger, loneliness, anxiety, fear, restlessness, and so on. The initial impulse, for the untrained practitioner, may be to fix or to eradicate the emotion, especially if it's unpleasant, to simply to feel better at that moment. But instead of fixing it, many meditative traditions teach us to *inhibit* the "fix it" response, and in so doing, we learn to stay with the experience, and even explore it with an attitude of curiosity.

For example, with anger, instead of trying to fix or to rid ourselves of the anger or figure out why we feel this way, we can learn to be present with our anger, exploring its various nuances of felt experience in the body, mind, and heart. We might note the underlying mental narrative going on along with the actual experience of the emotion of anger. This could include a narrative of blaming others or ourselves, or self-judgment, such as, "This isn't spiritual" or "I should be above this." We notice all these things.

As we learn to sit with our anger, and allow for the various thoughts and judgments around it to subside, we begin to see the experience more clearly, just as we see our reflections in the mirror for what they are, hear our voices, or feel our postures from within. We begin to see for ourselves how anger is actually very uncomfortable, and it's possible for something deep within us to self-correct, as if to say, "This isn't a good feeling."

In turn, change is *allowed* to happen, as if of its own accord, or from the inside out. It happens without a conscious efforting of "I'd better not be angry," but instead, more of a *relinquishing* of anger from seeing it more clearly for what it is. Some part of us correlates anger with this highly unpleasing experience, which it is, making the releasing of it a natural thing to do.

Here's an analogy: imagine becoming addicted to dog food due to a trauma of some kind. But when someone challenges you to pause in your eating and really taste the food, maybe you realize for the first time that it tastes bad. As you wake up to how bad it actually tastes, your preference for dog food naturally abates. There's no real conscious effort to stop eating dog food. It's more a matter of tasting it for real. I've found this principle helpful in working with many of the emotions usually classified under aversion, including fear and anger. Simply opening up to the *experience* of these mental/emotional states without trying to fix them has allowed me greater leverage in releasing them in the moment.

Whether it's eating dog food, working with our emotions, looking at our reflections, listening to our voices, or becoming aware of our postures, this same attitude and approach can be used when contemplating death. For example, if we are contemplating our potential death in 24 hours, and up comes "I want to be closer to my parents," we can apply the principle of inhibition to this impulse, which means we don't need to hop on the next flight to see them or to get on our phones immediately to call them. We might do this; but mostly, we can at least wait until we finish with our practice.

What we *can* do right away is simply bring our awareness to the yearning for closeness to our parents. It's the yearning that we want to notice and become more aware of in our lives.

By bringing light to these sometimes hidden yearnings and impulses that arise during contemplation of death, we're able to start making gradual changes in the daily choices we make. Using the example above, perhaps we find ourselves thinking of our parents more often, which in turn leads us to calling them more frequently, or sending them an email more often than before. It might also lead us to dropping other life commitments so we create more space in our lives for more visits. But it doesn't necessarily begin with a conscious intent to change our behavior. It comes about through greater awareness of the yearning to be closer.

Naturally, there are times when taking specific actions would be beneficial, but the practice is more about expanding one's awareness of what's truly going on underneath the surface of our everyday minds, and allowing for that increased awareness to naturally guide how we choose to live our lives. In this way, there isn't the constant *meddling* with living, but more a *relaxing into* living.

It's a path that leans on trust—that is, *trusting* a process rather than needing to *control* the process. In my experience of having tried both, I've found the former to be a much more effective, efficient, relaxed, and joyful path.

Exercise

The elder Western Theravada teacher, Stephen Levine, wrote the book, *A Year to Live*, in which he outlined a year-long experiment in contemplating one's death. The basic idea of his undertaking was to choose a start date and begin living as if he had exactly one year to live.

The following exercise is similar but instead of counting down from 365 to 0 days, we simply stay at 365 days left to live when we do the contemplation. Basically, it's the same exercise as the "24-hours left to live" exercise, but with an expanded time range.

In working with both the 24-hour range as well as the longer range of one-, three-, six-, or twelve-months, the kinds of issues that arise are qualitatively different enough that I consider them to be separate exercises. I've found for myself that three to six months oftentimes is the "sweet spot" that allows me to honestly confront where I'm living out of alignment with my deepest values. A full year feels too relaxed for my temperament, but perhaps you will find that a year is the perfect range for you to uncover aspects of yourself and your life that you may not have been confronting. My suggestion is that you experiment with one-, three-, then six-, then twelve-months, and see if you notice a particular range that triggers a sense of urgency toward change in your outer or inner life.

The format of this exercise is similar to the "24-hours left to live" one. Simply try to imagine that you have only n-months left to live (where n can be anything between one and twelve) and see how you might live differently under that scenario.

I encourage you to pause here in your reading and take a few minutes just to imagine this, and see what arises for you. You might consider jotting down some of your more prominent thoughts and emotions during this exercise.

Common reactions to this exercise that I've seen in myself and in others, are internal panic, an urge to travel and see the world, a desire to spend more time with loved ones, a questioning of why one isn't living more in alignment with one's deepest priorities and values, and a deepened spiritual impulse. There are many others. The most prominent issues to come up likely point to the places where we're not living as fully and deeply as we could be.

On Security

Sometimes in contemplating death—whether our own or others—an issue that can arise either directly, or more often in opposition to the ideas that arise, is that of security.

An example would be—*when I contemplate the fact that I am going to die in a year, I think to myself that I wouldn't be working at my current job. Instead, I would start a nonprofit center for inner-city children. But the reality is that I can't just quit my job and start something like that because I'm attached to the financial security of my current job.*

There are many other examples I've come across on this tension between pursuing what's meaningful and holding onto security. It's not my place here to preach the importance of pursuing what's meaningful, or to convince you to abandon security for meaning. I think that when such actions are taken without careful forethought or deliberation, they can backfire, both in terms of our overall well-being as well as our practice and consequent peace of mind.

Again, I want to call to mind the principle of inhibition. The contemplation of death is not about taking immediate action *necessarily*. It's about bringing into our awareness the different tensions that we hold within our psyche. What I've found in myself and in some of the people I have worked with is that in time, there's a recognition that the seeming security offered by unfulfilling situations eventually lose their importance to us, and in time, suffering through temporary instability allows us to move into a more deeply stable choice in the long run. When our approach is gradual and mindful like this, change can be experienced as gentle and natural, and much more swift and sustaining than a rushed and impulsive approach, ironically.

Under the regular and consistent awareness of death, security begins to be seen for what it is, illusory. From there, the pursuit of or holding onto it becomes less and less tenable, and in turn, can lead to a life of exhilarating yet frightening courage and aliveness. It's generally not wise to take actions when such understandings—that finding lasting security in things of this world is merely an illusion—are purely intellectual in nature. It has to sink in deeper. We have to bring the repetitive technology of contemplative meditation of death to bear upon our psyche, so as to bring the true awareness of the illusory nature of security deep into our beings.

Then, when we hear about a downsizing at our work, for example, we don't panic to quite the same degree. We recognize that this is the nature of things. If we protest the downsizing, it comes from a place of understanding or compassion for others, rather than from a frightened part of us that clings to security.

Maybe we also begin to see that our pursuit of wealth is misguided after the point of comfort. How much do we truly need in order to live comfortably? What is comfortable? Research shows that in the US, an annual salary of around $75,000 per person is optimally correlated with happiness. In comparison, in a country like Indonesia, the average monthly salary may be somewhere between $150 - $250/month in many places, and yet, many of these same people appear happy and contented. Those who have more sometimes feel that they need more. For some of us, the more we make, the higher we set the bar for ourselves financially. Is this peace?

The Deeper Fruits

Imagine practicing this exercise daily over a few weeks or months. You would likely see a slow yet steady transformation in your life, even without conscious efforting at change itself. Think back to the principle of inhibition. Simply by bringing certain otherwise-buried issues into the light of our awareness, we bring the possibility of true transformation into our lives.

I've found that contemplating death in these various ways across a year led me to slowly adopt lifestyle changes to the point, where now, there is very little I would do differently if I had only three to twelve months to live. It's perhaps a good indication that I'm living in sync with my deeper values, insofar as my worldly existence is concerned.

Where I still feel a hitch, though, is in the realm of spiritual practice, which (as I have already mentioned) is where the contemplation of death is ultimately meant to direct our attention. It's one thing to temporarily "straighten out" one's life, which actually may be a misnomer. It's not so much that one's life gets straightened out, but that one comes to recognize that outside of a few fundamental needs, such as food, water, shelter, warmth, some level of connection and contribution, there's little lasting meaning or fulfillment in pursuing and filling one's life with countless "worldly" activities. So, it's more like a mental and emotional paring, if you will.

It's not that one gets rid of things, though that can be part of it. It's more a recognition that there isn't a whole lot that's important other than coming to see more clearly and learning to rest in a state of trust and peace. One needn't "straighten" everything out for there to be peace. Perhaps some relationships can be mended, for example, but there can also be deep acceptance and peace in broken relationships, as well as in the sadness that may accompany such relationships.

As we contemplate death further and deeper, the changes also begin to move further into our own lives and lifestyle. They begin to permeate our fundamental attitude toward who we are and how we interact with others. Then, perhaps, the words of Geshe Polowa begin to resonate to our experience:

> *Think about death and impermanence for a long time. Once you are certain that you are going to die, you will no longer find it hard to put aside harmful actions nor difficult to do what is right.*[24]

The more real our death as well as the death of others becomes to us, the more silly our squabbles and fights seem. We might begin to ask, "Would I really care about being right if one of us were to die tonight?" Under the light of death, many of our preoccupations such as these become pointless, which is to see many of them for what they truly are. In turn, it becomes natural to do what we know to be right, whether genuinely moving past our anger toward the love inside of us, or giving up harmful habits for helpful ones.

What these contemplations on death seem to do is bring up the things left unexamined in the heart, starting at the surface. As we address and bring

---

[24] Credit: Patrul Rinpoche, excerpts from *The Words of My Perfect Teacher,* translated by the Padmakara Translation Group. Copyright © 1994, 1998 by Padmakara Translation Group. Reprinted with the permission of The Permissions Company, Inc., on behalf of Shambhala Publications Inc., Boulder, Colorado, www.shambhala.com.

some level of resolution to them, deeper aspects of our hearts begin to surface, and in this way, we go deeper and deeper.

When we get to the deepest parts of our hearts, we arrive at the sacred, most profound spiritual impulses within ourselves. We are then turned toward the Dharma, toward the spiritual, or that which calls us toward the greatest and most expansive freedom imaginable.

—Week eight

We'll continue to focus on expanding the middle.

In case there's too much a sense of morbidity with this continuous focus on death, it might be worth noting that for many Buddhists, life is sometimes conceived as a long preparation for the moment of death.

One other thing: if you're a verbally-oriented person, it can be helpful to write the verse in question or a succinct description of the exercise (e.g., "Contemplate your death in three months") on a piece of paper and place it directly in front of you during the meditation period. This can act as an anchor to your thinking. If you're like me, you might easily fly off on irrelevant tangents (such as daydreaming about the day to come), but can always come back to it since it's written right in front of you.

Preliminary:
1. Set time and place.
2. Relaxed and upright posture; allow for some settling.

Beginning:
3. Refuge.
4. Bodhicitta.

Middle:
5. Timer set to **five minutes** and practice shamatha for those five minutes.
6. Re-set the timer to **seven minutes,** and engage in one of the following three contemplative exercises, or some combination:
     1. Take the line "*Whatever is born is impermanent and is bound to die*" and use that as the basis for contemplation.
     2. Repeat the "24 hours to live" exercise from the last chapter.
     3. Repeat the "*n* months to live" exercise from this chapter. You might experiment with different values for *n,* such as one month, three months, six months, nine months, all the way up to a full year.

Toward the end of the time, relax into the state of being that your reflecting produces in you. So we're aiming for about **12 total minutes of practice time!**

Ending:
7. Offer merit.

Chapter 14: On the impermanence of that which we can acquire or possess

We've spent the past three weeks contemplating death in one form or another. The first line of the larger verse we're working with (*"Whatever is born is impermanent and is bound to die"*) has to do with existence: birth and death, being and non-being.

Here's the second line: *Whatever is stored up is impermanent and is bound to run out.*

Before proceeding further, pause in your reading and briefly contemplate the meaning of this line for yourself.

The line speaks to things that we can store up, acquire, have or possess. While the first line says, what *exists* is impermanent and will cease to exist, this line says that whatever can be *had* is impermanent by nature, and we can't have it forever. It runs out.

So we're attending to another dimension of living, from existence itself to what we can acquire and possess.

Maybe the first thing that comes to mind when we read this line is money? We know that we can store up all the money we want, but at some point it'll either run out on us, or we'll die and it'll become useless to us. This doesn't mean that we should then become spendthrifts and throw our money away just because it can't be stored up forever. But knowing the truth of its impermanence in our hearts may help us cling less to our finances, allowing things just to be as they are. Our grip on our finances may loosen, not so much in the direction of buying more and more things (which in itself could be a futile attempt at further storing), but in the practice of generosity. There may even come a sense of relief from this.

If you are ecologically-minded, your thoughts might turn to the natural resources such as water or energy. Unless we keep storing more, they will run out, and even that is no guarantee.

The line can also be thought of in terms of knowledge. How many of us accrue and go about gathering knowledge, whether within formal settings such as academia, or through reading large amounts of books, blogs, and the like? Certainly, some of it stays with us, but much of it fades, not just from conscious awareness but even in terms of how it influences our behavior or decision-making. Again, this doesn't mean that we want to remain ignorant and fail to grow in our learning. But it does call our attention to being more mindful of whether we are gathering knowledge simply for its own accumulation, or because we truly want to learn something deeply and participate in the act of creation borne of that gathering.

Some of us try to have as many different experiences as possible, becoming in the process, experiential gluttons, if you will. The attitude is that by having many different experiences, we'll create many memories to cherish for a long time. And yet, even those memories fade. They too will run out in time.

On a spiritual level, the line also points to the nature of our karma. We may engage in virtuous deeds and accumulate good karma, but even that will run out eventually. In fact, it's taught within the Bodhidharma that whatever "good" we're enjoying will last only until our "good" karma runs out. Once it does, then the seemingly good circumstances will fade despite all intentions and attempts to make it otherwise, and thus, we cannot rest on our spiritual laurels.

These faded periods are often called "dry spells," which from the karmic perspective are simply times without sufficient karma for the dry spell to come to an end. If we want to change our circumstances, we change our actions to produce the desired karmic outcome. If we desire greater wealth, we practice material generosity. If we desire greater emotional safety, we practice emotional generosity by practicing patience and ethical behavior that considers the welfare and well-being of others. And if we desire greater spiritual insight, we practice spiritual generosity as in sharing our spiritual insights—such as the Dharma—with others.

Buddhist cosmology teaches that there are realms other than the earthly one we're familiar with. One of these is the "God realm," where one is reborn out of good deeds. But even there, once the karma that landed one in such a wonderful place runs out, it's game over. One is sent back to a lower realm. It's said that the good karma runs out because living there is so good and wishes come true easily, and so one stops doing the good deeds that brought them there in the first place. On a less esoteric level, this might be equated to becoming a multi-millionaire CEO or rock star. With all the money, power, adulation and all, what motive is there to go out into the world and do good deeds, practice meditation every day, and so on? Eventually, whatever good karma brought oneself there runs out, and the whole thing fades.

Without the trappings of Buddhism, but within the context of a general spirituality, the line we are examining in this chapter can be understood as follows: Without feeding our spiritual practice, our spiritual conditioning goes away. In short, we can't rest on our spiritual laurels in spite of whatever accomplishments we may have at the moment.

In a general sense, whenever we turn something into an object that can be possessed, this line is relevant. So for example, in the English language when we say, "You are my friend," we've turned a person into a possession, at least conceptually, through that linguistic turn. We even say, "I have many friends," as if people are things to be had. This becomes more acutely relevant when we think of "Facebook friends," which the website counts for us automatically. Some have thousands of such friends, as if friends were quantifiable objects.

When we think of others as "my" friends, the line has relevance and resonance, as if we were storing up friends in our minds. And of course, they "run out" also. Friends come and go, whether they enter and exit our lives as friends across years, or connect and part until the next meeting, across days.

In this manner, this line points to the impermanence of all the things we can turn into an actual or conceptual possession.

Ego as Our Set of Preferences

Related to our karma or habitual tendencies, is the notion of ego. While there are a number of ways to conceptualize the ego, one of them is to think of it as the collection of our preferences.

The beloved Buddhist nun and writer, Pema Chodron, has written of the ego as being like a room set to our preferences, playing our favorite music, painted in our favorite colors, and decorated with our favorite things. Only the people we like and want with us are in our special room. All that we don't like stays out.

Chodron goes on to remark that living a life based upon ego is similar to keeping *in* what we like and keeping *out* what we don't like from this room of ours. *In other words, a life based upon ego is a life based upon our preferences. And naturally, our preferences are little more than conditioned and habituated patterns of mind.* Living this way, she remarks, can make one's life smaller and smaller, as we'll strive to hold onto those things we find pleasant and desirable and *keep out* all that we find unpleasant and undesirable. Because life itself simply *is*, our constant attempts at clinging to what we want while filtering out what we don't, closes us off from the richness and fullness that life is. In fact, Chodron describes the spiritual life as one of *slowly* putting holes in the walls of this room of ego, so as to allow what we cling to to possibly escape, and to allow in what we don't like or want. In this way we learn to make peace with what life has to offer and take from us.

When we think of ego in this way, we can see it as nothing more than our *accumulated* habits of preference. The line for this chapter, then, points to the impermanence of our stored-up preferences, that is, to ego itself. It reminds us that our preferences are not set in stone by any means, and that they too are transient.

Perhaps you can think of preferences that have faded or even switched to their opposites in the course of your life? Maybe you have a friend or lover who you once held as a stranger, or even an enemy? Or vice versa. Maybe you've noticed changes in your preferences for food or music? These are all simply habits of mind, after all. *They can be conditioned as well as de-conditioned.* In other words our ego, as construed in this way, is impermanent and subject to de-conditioning, which should come as a great relief for most of us. *It speaks to an innate capacity for liberating ourselves from our egoistic tendencies or preferences.* We can move toward a more open manner of interacting with reality itself, which doesn't seem to care one bit whether our likes and dislikes are met or not.

When our likes and dislikes are less vocal in our minds, as if receding into the background, we're then free to live our lives more in accordance with the way things are. Loosening our attachments to our preferences affords us this profound freedom.

Even in something as sensually pleasurable, and almost universally-*preferred*, as love making, one can become aware and mindful of what's going on in the mind and in the heart, or in the entirety of the experience. Observe carefully and you will become aware of deep pleasure, connection, and feelings of fulfillment, and at the same time, you may notice a persistent thread of dissatisfaction, perhaps experienced as a yearning for something more, based upon the ever-present awareness of the impermanence of the experience. When we practice this kind of discriminatory seeing, instead of glossing over the nuances of the experience and pretending to ourselves that it's all good, we introduce the slightest element of doubt in our attachment to this form of sensual pleasure.

Every experience, as taught by the Buddha, has a thread of dissatisfaction as well as impermanence running through it. This "dissatisfaction" is more often termed stress or suffering, or in Sanskrit, *dukkha*. Suffering and impermanence constitute two of the three characteristics inherent in all experienced phenomena, as taught by the Buddha. The third is *anata,* or non-self, which can be thought of as a localized version of emptiness, which I will discuss later in this book.

There's a part of us that knows and is aware that no experience we have can last. As we bring this awareness into our consciousness and our lives, we gradually reduce our clinging and see into the impermanence of all experiences. This doesn't mean we become less happy and joyful. Our joy is simply tempered by more realistic expectations, and through this tempering, we experience less shocks to our system that would inadvertently shut us down to the happiness and joy available to us in every moment.

The purpose of these contemplations on impermanence is to encourage the letting go of our clinging, whether to money, to things, to friends, to sex, even to our likes and dislikes. Of the three poisons (attachment, aversion, and ignorance), attachment is the poison these contemplations primarily address.

What oftentimes presents itself as the primary obstacle to establishing a daily practice is our attachments, whether it be our clinging to the world in the form of sensual desires, distractions, or to our own ego and its stories. As we begin to allow the thought of impermanence to permeate our minds, we slowly begin to see through our attachments and are able to let go ever so slightly. In doing so, it's not that we become disgusted by everything and in turn averse to living, but instead we become more weary with seeking fulfillment through transitory phenomena that characterize much of our "worldly" pursuits. We see a little more clearly that they lack stable fulfillment and happiness, and from there, we turn ever more so slightly toward a spiritual solution, or to the Dharma.

Preliminary:
1. Set time and place.
2. Relaxed and upright posture; allow for some settling.

Beginning:
3. Refuge.
4. Bodhicitta.

Middle:
5. Set timer to **five minutes** and practice shamatha for those five minutes.
6. Re-set the timer to **ten minutes,** and engage in one of the following two contemplative exercises, or some combination:

I. Take the line *"Whatever is stored up is impermanent and is bound to run out"* and use that as the basis for contemplation. Here are some questions to consider during your contemplation. You might just stay with one set of questions per day (as there are exactly seven):

1) Where in your life might you be holding onto *things*? Can you see how that very thing you hold onto is not permanent? When you contemplate the impermanence of that which you hold onto, what arises in your mind and in your heart? Stay with what arises, whether it be sadness, fear, anxiety, and so on.

2) What is your relationship to money? Do you tend to hoard and be obsessive or compulsive about making more and more, as if there were no end? Combine this inquiry with the one on death. Can you see that having enough to be comfortable might truly be enough? In fact, what is your relationship to the attitude and feeling of contentment? Where are you oftentimes content, and where are you discontent? Examine your relationship to these areas through the lens of impermanence—that is, do you tend to secretly hold onto some longing for permanence in those areas where you are more often discontented?

3) How do you hold friends in your mind and heart? Are you focused on *being* a friend or do you think more in terms of *having* or not *having* friends? Can you

imagine a reality where you *have* no friends, but you're a friend to those you encounter? Does this bring up feelings of scarcity or freedom for you? Is it necessary for you to "have" friends? Can you truly have them, or is this a social contract? Is a social contract a true friendship?

4) What is your relationship to knowledge, to information, and to ideas? Do you tend to accumulate knowledge or ideas for their own sake? What is your reason for this? Is it to buttress your sense of identity? Or is there a further purpose?

5) What is your relationship to experiences themselves? Just as some people try to accumulate knowledge for its own sake, others try to accumulate memories for their own sake through having many diverse experiences. What is the purpose of this? Does it truly lead to greater freedom? Or can this too be a kind of trap or pursuit without end, a distraction from seeking a higher freedom?

6) What is your relationship to your spirituality, and in particular, to your spiritual accomplishments? Do you have a

tendency to rest on your spiritual laurels? Do you ever suffer from compla-
cency? If so, do you expect your
current streak of good fortune or happiness to continue without further
work? Can you see the possibility that
the merit from past work might run out
at any time? Can you see the truth of
this in your life? What does this bring
up for you?

7) What is your relationship to your personal preferences? Do you see them as
somehow ingrained and permanent? Can you think of instances of
when they changed or shifted? Can
you think of instances where they
flipped around to their opposites? If
you can, and if you can see your preferences as malleable, what might that
mean to you in terms of living your life
based upon your personal preferences? How might your personal preferences be limiting you in your choices
in life? Do you choose based around
your personal preferences even when
they might conflict with deeply-held
values or (spiritual) principles? Or are
you able to make your choices based
upon principles over your own preferences when they are in conflict with

one another? Can you see how choosing based upon principles can oftentimes open up our lives out of our comfort zone, while choosing based upon preferences can many times keep our lives smaller?

II.   If you feel compelled to stay with the contemplation on death from the past three weeks, you might choose to do so.

Toward the end of the time, relax into the state of being that reflecting produces in you. So we're aiming for about **15 total minutes of practice time!**

Ending:
7. Offer merit.

Chapter 15: Impermanence of connections

We're now at the third line: *Whatever comes together is impermanent and is bound to come apart.*

When you read this line, what comes to mind?

Perhaps it's the transient nature of our relationships? If we examine our past, we might notice how many of our friendships have come and gone, not to speak of countless acquaintances. We come together, and oftentimes for reasons beyond our control, we come apart. The same might be said for some of our intimate relationships.

If we think about our friendships in regards to this phrase, maybe we feel a sense of peace about things

without guilt or blame? Instead of thinking of a parting as a reflection of our own or the other's short-
comings as a friend or partner, we might just accept
things for how they are. The coming apart becomes
less about what someone has or hasn't done; it's oftentimes less personal than that.

On another level, the line alludes to the compounded
nature of all things. Because all things of this world
are compounded or aggregated in nature, they'll tend
eventually to disaggregate and to disperse. In this
way, no "thing" lasts forever in its current state,
whether it's a car, a mountain, or a piece of
metal. The fact that it fails to last forever is precisely
due to its compounded nature, in that all objects in
this reality are compounded phenomena, and because
they're aggregates of smaller things that have come
together, they must come apart.

For example, if you examine a pen, you might note
that it's constituted by different parts, such as the
plastic encasing, the ink holder, the metallic tip, the
clip for binding to a shirt pocket, and so on. Each of
these parts is made up of smaller parts; for example,
the ink in the ink holder is made up of ink molecules,
and each of these molecules consists of atoms, which
are made up of electrons, protons, and neutrons, and
so on and so forth.

Viewed in this light, a pen is simply a conglomera-
tion of many different things that have temporarily
come together in time to form this object that we call

a pen. We might even say that "pen" is nothing more than a mental fabrication that we overlay on this temporary configuration of atoms, molecules, and so on, or that which is the basic constituent element of it all, which is sometimes referred to in the Dharma as "light" or "energy."

To further clarify mental fabrication, consider a cloud formation that for just one moment looks like a dragon, and for that one moment, you forget that it's a cloud. In that moment, you can call it a dragon if you like, but that would be nothing more than a mental imputation upon some clouds. It's a temporary label or concept that you're overlaying upon the cloud formation. You've simply forgotten for that moment that you're looking at a cloud.

Similarly, when we look at a pen, we forget that we're simply looking at a collection of atoms, or spinning electrons. And though the time scale is different between a cloud formation looking like a dragon for one moment and a collection of atoms looking and feeling like a pen for many years, the difference in time scale doesn't change the reality that what we call a pen is nothing more than a temporary configuration of atomic "clouds." We can reside in that forgetting for the entirety of our lives, or we can remind ourselves, "Hey, this isn't a dragon. It looks like one, but it's really just some moving clouds," or in our case, moving energy or atoms.

In this way, any and all objects can be seen for what they are—compounded phenomena existing temporarily in their current configuration. They're not fixed objects with some intrinsic existence as an independently-existing thing, but rather, they're a gathering of energy or atoms temporarily brought together by an infinite number of "external-to-itself" causes and conditions.

We can begin to peer into these infinite number of causes and conditions that constitute an object such as a pen, by asking this question—*what brought these many things together in this object we call a pen?*

Perhaps factory workers built machinery that produced these pens—factory workers whose existence depended upon their own parents being alive, which was made possible by farmers who grew food that nourished them. And that's just one narrow line of causality. If one traces back all the causes that give rise to a pen, an infinite number of interdependent lines of causality can be seen to converge upon the pen that sits in front of us right now. We can sense an inkling of the miracle that is a pen when we begin to fathom how many events had to conspire for that pen simply to come into being.

Similarly, we are like this pen, a temporary configuration of light or energy, having arisen due to a countless number of causes and conditions, constituted by a gazillion parts and pieces that have come together and will one day come apart.

Even something as simple as the act of breathing means that something or some event had to produce oxygen for us to breathe, not to mention the complex interaction and coordination that has to take place in our bodies for a single breath to occur. If we think of eating a piece of fruit, the actions that had to occur for that fruit to enter our mouths are countless. Put it all together in a typical day in the life of any of us, and the web of interactions necessary for a day to happen are overwhelmingly complex and astounding. If even one of those actions had failed to occur, we may not even exist as we are! On top of it, the string of events would go all the way back to the very beginning of time, supposing that such an event truly existed.

If we view ourselves as many constituent parts brought together and sustained by the infinite number of actions of others, as well as events, we begin to experience a glimpse of the *interdependent* nature of who we are. We don't exist independent of the web of actions taking place around us. In fact, one would be hard-pressed to find any aspect of ourselves that independently exists outside the web, thereby problematizing the whole notion of who the "self" (as independent in itself) truly is.

This notion of interdependence is another word for the oft-bandied about Buddhist concept of *emptiness*. We may think in our minds that we exist independently, and yet, every single part of our bodies, our thoughts, our emotions, even what we consider our consciousness, has arisen through actions occurring outside of (what we normally consider) ourselves. In this way, there is no part of this thing called "self" that can be considered intrinsic to itself, or independent of anything "outside" of itself. Since every single aspect of this self is in this way interdependent, then there is no such thing as an intrinsic self, or a self that is independent unto itself. This is why Buddhists say that the "self is empty." What is meant is that the self is empty of any intrinsic, independent nature that we would otherwise call self.

And this is why *interdependence* and *emptiness* are phenomenal synonyms for one another.

When it comes to the interdependent nature of our bodies, scientific research suggests that many of our cells are sloughed off and replaced by new ones at varying rates. If so many of our cells are continually being replaced, can we truly say that this is truly *my* body? Perhaps it would be more accurate to say that it's my *current* and *temporary* body (although "my" is problematic here since one could question who that self is)?

Similarly, our thoughts arise and fade dependent upon external and internal stimuli, as do our emotions since they're entwined with our thoughts. Even consciousness arises in relation to, or *in contact* with an object. Without an object to contact, there is no consciousness, at least as argued in the Abhidharma, a Buddhist psychological text. If one were to think of consciousness as self, we could simply restate this as, *without the other and contact with this other, there is no self.* This isn't far from what the theologian Martin Buber suggests when he says *the self is defined in relationship.* It's in this contact with other—the relationship itself—that self arises and is defined. It's not that there's an intrinsically-defined self that meets with another intrinsically-defined self and forms a relationship, but rather the opposite. The relationship defines the co-participants. Hence, *a self exists only in concept and in interdependence with what appears "outside" of itself.* And yet, due to the interdependent nature of all phenomena, what appears to be on the "outside" is simply an *appearance* and not necessarily the truth of things. The truth of things is more along the lines of an interplay or dance of light, energy, consciousness, and form.

We are of an interdependent nature as are all other things of this phenomenal world. No thing exists independently of this web of interconnectedness.

A common metaphor used to illustrate this is to consider the ocean as the web of all interconnected phenomena, and a wave as any seeming "self" or thing within this web. A wave rises in this ocean, and right at its crest, we imagine the wave gaining self-consciousness and thinking, "Hey, I'm a wave! I have independent existence!" Then soon, "Oh no! I'm going to crash and die into oblivion!" Of course the wave is a part of the ocean the entire time, just as we are said to be part of the interconnected ocean of all phenomena.

In this way, we are interconnected at all times, even without our acknowledgement or knowing, and yet, the surface is always undulating, changing. It's on the surface that we appear to connect and to part, but even when apart, we are always a part of phenomenal reality, the large ocean of existence and nonexistence.

The line, *whatever comes together is impermanent and is bound to come apart,* then points to the impermanence of *seeming* connections that occur within the larger soup of reality. Whether it's molecules coming together as part of a compounded object, or of relationships coming together, there is a seeming coming together and a seeming parting. When the causes and conditions that would give rise to a coming together are removed, then parting occurs, things come apart.

This sort of contemplation upon the compounded nature of all things and their impermanent nature is addressed in the *Vinaya* by the Buddha:

To remember for an instant the imperma-
nence of all compounded things is greater
than giving food and offerings to a hundred
of any disciples who are perfect vessels.[25]

In the teachings on karma, we learn to gather favora-
ble karma through acts of generosity. The degree of
the merit that is accumulated depends upon a number
of factors, one of the more important being the recip-
ient of our act. Giving food to a rich man who already has plenty is considered less meritorious on a
karmic level than giving to someone who is poor and
starving. Giving to our own parents is considered
higher than to someone else. But giving to the three
jewels—the Buddha, the Dharma, or to the Sangha—
is considered the highest of all, and within the
Sangha, it is the most adept and highly accomplished
of disciples—i.e., those who are "perfect vessels"—
who are considered the ideal recipients of our offerings.

In this way, giving food and offerings to not just one
but a hundred of these disciples who are perfect vessels is of the highest merit that one can imagine, and
yet, a momentary contemplation upon the impermanence of all compounded phenomena is considered
higher.

Why might this be? Perhaps it is because the contemplation upon impermanence begins to put the

---

[25] Ibid.

slightest chink in the armor of delusion that things here have permanence? And this little break in the delusion is what can lead to a life of practice that eventually culminates in true liberation. Giving to these great beings leads to profound happiness and further riches, but they are temporary satisfactions and pale in comparison to the peace of true liberation.

In Relationship

As with the previous contemplations, this line isn't intended to encourage us to become hermits and to avoid relationships just because all forms of coming-together result in a coming apart. It's more so we don't come into them with unrealistic expectations that defy the nature of reality. We can engage more authentically and with greater presence when we don't enter into relationships with an attitude of, "I want this relationship to last forever or it's not worth it!" No, the nature of these things is that we connect and then we come apart. We may do so in a few minutes, a few hours, a few weeks, a few years, or a few lifetimes. We may also come back together in a few minutes all the way to a few lifetimes later.

Having an awareness of the impermanent nature of relationships is to see things for what they are, which helps us to relax in our attitude and in our approach since we're not resisting the true nature of reality.

Even if we're in a life-long marriage, or have a very close relationship with our children for the entirety of our lives, the *quality* of connection is impermanent. That is, we can examine the microscopic elements of our being together. If we do so, we'll easily notice that even in the span of a minute, the connection isn't stable or steady. It wavers since all things are constantly in flux. This isn't a bad thing. It's the simple reality of our relationships, that there's a continual ebb and flow even to all "sustaining" relationships.

When we stop fighting the ebb and flow nature of our relationships, and begin accepting them for what they are, we see that basing our happiness in terms of a perpetual feeling of closeness and connection to another is foolhardy and stressful. When we learn to let the coming together and the coming apart occur as they are, we find the possibility for real peace in regards to relationship. We are then seeing and accepting the reality of relationships for what they are, and in this, there is always deeper peace.

One thing that can hinder us in accepting the ebb and flow nature of relationships is an unwelcomeness within ourselves toward feeling sadness and grief. Although I already wrote of sadness in a prior chapter, I think it's important to mention again here.

We can accept in our *minds* the transient nature of relationships, and yet, on an emotional level, many of us still experience the typical highs and lows that come with entering into and parting from an intimate partner. In other words, accepting the reality of parting doesn't preclude us from experiencing the accompanying joy and excitement as well as the sadness and grief, in particular.

While the grieving process is said to involve denial and anger, in its "cleanest" or least neurotic manifestation—at least as I have seen it in myself and others close to me—the accompanying emotion to parting *at its core* is simply sadness.

I've found that accepting the temporary nature of relationships is tantamount to accepting, on an emotional level, the regular nature of sadness. That is to say, the more I come to peace with and embrace the experience of sadness, the more deeply I'm able to rest into the ebb and flow nature of relationships. My prior resistance—or greater resistance to be more accurate—stemmed from an uncomfortable relationship to the emotion of sadness.

When I'm uncomfortable with my own sadness, unwilling to feel it for what it is and to embrace the emotion, I'm bereft of the capacity to be at peace in the partings of life. Either I must abscond into my head with unconvincing rationalizations (i.e., "I knew it wouldn't last anyway.")—"unconvincing" because I remain un-joyous and/or emotionally disengaged at living—or else, I refrain from fully involving myself into a future relationship for fear of the impending parting, which would mean more sadness. It's similar to someone who has an uncomfortable relationship to anger, and thus, avoids revealing his or her true feelings in close relationships for fear of conflict, which could trigger his or her own anger.

In this way, contemplation on the impermanent nature of that which comes together can bring us face-to-face with our own relationship to grief and sadness.

Preliminary:
1. Set time and place.
2. Relaxed and upright posture; allow for some settling.

Beginning:
3. Refuge.
4. Bodhicitta.

Middle:
5. Set timer to **five minutes** and practice shamatha
for those five minutes.
6. Re-set the timer to **twelve minutes,** then use the
line *"Whatever comes together is impermanent
and is bound to come apart"* as the basis for contemplation, and consider these questions. You
might try each of them, or stay on any one of
them that leads to any kind of deepening.

   a) Contemplation on the compounded nature of
   all phenomena (Part 1): Take a look around
   and pick any object. In your mind, separate it

into its constituent parts. Do this with every object that your eyes alight upon. Although this may feel mechanical, you're training yourself to see into the true nature of things. If you persist at this exercise, you'll gradually begin to feel and sense the unsolidity of things around you, which can result in a more relaxed feeling within yourself. Something worth thinking about is this: It's a known fact that the world is round, and yet, to our eyes, it looks flat in every direction. We know due to our educational training that what the eyes see isn't the true story of the shape of the ground beneath us. Similarly, our eyes tell us we're surrounded by solid objects, but if we train ourselves to see the constituent parts of all objects, the result is a stronger knowing of the unsolidity of all things. This is one way we can come to live in *truer knowing* as opposed to being deceived by our senses.

b) Contemplation on the compounded nature of all phenomena (Part 2): Take a look around and pick any object. In your mind, think of one event that was necessary for this object to exist as it is. Then, think of another event that was necessary for that other event to occur. Trace backwards in time from one event to the one before. Go back as far as you can. Then, start with the same object but trace back through another line of causality. Continue doing this as a mental exercise with any and all objects in your field of perception. You might include yourself among these objects. The idea is to practice training the mind into seeing the interdependent nature of all phenomena. We're trying to make conscious that which may be implicit, and thus hidden, for many of us.

c) Examine your relationship to people, places, and things on a larger scale, across years. Think of how people have come and gone in your life. Think of how places and things have come and gone as well. How do you react inwardly? If sadness arises, stay with it for the duration of the practice session. Or maybe it's anger or disappointment you feel? Whatever it may be, try staying with the emotion, allowing yourself to feel what arises. Think of these feelings as having been unfelt in your heart for a long time, and through this contemplation, they've arisen in your psyche. Now it's time for you to feel them, and as you do, you're liberating them in order to liberate that part of your heart that's been holding onto them. You might be inclined to journal on those feelings afterwards. If you feel called to do so, you might consider staying with this contemplation for a few days, or even an additional week if there's enough emotional "charge" to this contemplation for you.

d) Examine your relationship to people, places, and things on a smaller scale, across moments. Recall past episodes of platonic or romantic intimacy. Notice how you can be intimate with another in one moment, only to come apart in the subtlest way the next? Can you see it as a part of the ebb and flow of relating rather than taking it personally? What do you learn about yourself and the nature of things when you think back upon these moments and their impermanent nature at a micro-level?

Although outside the scope of formal sitting meditation, an interesting place to practice this awareness is during any act of intimacy with another. If you happen to have the opportunity, the next time that you're intimate with another—whether in an intimate conversation or in love making—try making a commitment to paying attention to the ebb and flow of intimacy, to the coming together and parting that's part of the dance of interaction or love making. Notice how you move with that flow. How do you react when you come together? And how do you react when there is the momentary parting? Do you try to change it, or move it back closer? Can you notice the part of you that clings to closeness,

and how much trusting there is that the coming together will occur again? Can you see
that in even in the pleasurable nature of love
making, there is room for clinging, dissatisfaction, and other such forms of suffering
(which is what the Buddha taught)? You can
learn a lot about your attachments and your
relationship to pleasure by watching your
mind during moments of intimacy with someone.

Another possibility is in the practice of ne-
otantra, where two lovers simply look into
one another's eyes without any overt sexual
contact. One can bring an awareness of the
impermanence of coming together into this
practice, noticing the ebb and flow dynamics
as described in the previous paragraph. When you look into the eyes of a
lover, there's the same dynamic of intimacy
and distance, back and forth. Can you move
with this instead of forcing things or telling
yourself that there's only closeness?

e) You might use any of the contemplations
    above to help gauge your relationship to sad-
    ness or grief. What is your relationship to
    this particular emotion? If you're a male in
    Western culture, there is a likelihood that you
    have an easier time acknowledging and ex-
    pressing anger than sadness. (It's commonly

the opposite for women in Western culture.) Is this true for you? Is it more common for you to feel anger (including frustration, impatience, irritation, annoyance, and so on) than for you to feel and acknowledge sadness (including grief, loneliness, melancholia, and so on)? If so, you might inquire as to why you have a resistance to feeling sadness and its accompanying constellation of emotions? What beliefs might you carry about yourself or about reality that keep you from fully feeling sadness in your life? What would it mean to be someone who feels a lot of sadness? Can you come to the point of simply feeling sadness as another emotion, and even come to see the beauty of it?

Toward the end of the time, relax into the state of being that reflecting produces in you. We're aiming for about **17 total minutes of practice time!** If you've been keeping pace, you're almost at the goal of 21 minutes a day!

Ending:
7. Offer merit.

Chapter 16: The impermanence of that which is built

Here's the fourth line: *Whatever is built is impermanent and is bound to collapse.*

Here, we might first think of objects such as buildings and bridges. There are also empires and civilizations, such as the Roman Empire or even the current US civilization. Certainly, none of these things are lasting, at least in their past or current forms.

For those of us who create or are artists, there is the art we build. That too is bound toward impermanence, and we know this deep inside, and yet, how many of us cling to the idea of our work having a lasting and permanent quality? If you do, you probably know already the tightness of mind in such an attitude and how it can constrain creativity.

On the other hand, there are artists such as Andy Goldsworthy, featured in the movie *Rivers and Tides*, who work explicitly in mediums intended to decay and disappear within nature. There are also the Tibetan artists (many of them monks) who construct intricate sand mandalas that are typically swept away in ceremony upon completion. To create without holding onto any sense of permanence is simply to recognize the true nature of creation, and as such, is perhaps a more freeing attitude to adopt in creative pursuits than to cling to some want of *lasting* accomplishment.

We also *build* our reputations and status in society. According to Dharma teachings, these too are subject to collapse or loss. The Buddha's teachings on the *eight worldly winds* are particularly relevant here. Imagine standing on an open hillside, and a cool breeze blows. Chances are the breeze will touch your skin; you'll feel that cool wind. The only way to avoid being touched by the various winds is either to wrap yourself up like a mummy so no part of you is exposed, or never to venture outside. Neither possibility is a realistic option for a healthy person wanting to live a normal life.

The eight worldly winds are paired as follows: pleasure and pain; gain and loss; praise and blame; fame and disrepute. These eight qualities are like the breezes that blow in our natural world. As long as you're alive and living a regular sort of life, it's taught that you can expect to be touched by them. They're impersonal factors that come into all of our lives. When we feel pain, loss, blame, or disrepute, it's not necessarily a personal attack on who we are. It just is. It's a natural part of the experience of living.

We can free ourselves from unhealthy self-judgments when we accept the impersonal nature of these worldly winds. It's the same with pleasure, gain, praise, and fame. These aren't particularly personal either. They're no reason to get on an ego trip. Certainly, it's influenced by one's karma (actions), but even the Buddha himself suffered from pain, loss, blame, and even disrepute in his lifetime (his own brother tried to kill him after his enlightenment)!

If we consider these eight worldly winds for what they are, then we also free ourselves from the compulsive need to attaching ourselves to the pleasant ones and avoiding the unpleasant ones. And yet, how many of us live our lives contrary to this, in constant pursuit of more pleasure, gain, praise, and fame, while doggedly trying our best to avoid pain, loss, blame, and disrepute? What if instead we were to live our lives guided by principles such as humility, kindness, service and the like, accepting that we would experience our share of the eight winds? Wouldn't that be a profound freedom?

It's taught that our reputations (fame) and status (praise) are not stable things that we can hold onto. They too collapse, and as such, there is no peace to be found in clutching onto them. So we contemplate the impermanent nature of our reputation and status as part of this contemplation.

There is also our spiritual practice. I've used the word "build" in the title of this book. Many of us who aspire toward deeper spiritual growth have a practice we've built. Or we might say that we're "building" our spiritual muscles. And yet, even these collapse in a matter of speaking. In fact, one might even say that this is the whole point of spiritual practice.

In spiritual circles, we often hear the idea of giving up one's ego. But to give up an ego, there has to be an ego to begin with that's worth giving up. Or so I was taught by an elder friend who also happened to be a therapist. Most people who come into 12-step programs are beaten down to the point where they exemplify a lyric made famous by Janis Joplin— "Freedom's just another word for nothing left to lose." But that isn't true freedom; it's sheer desperation and bottoming-out. True freedom is a *conscious* letting go that's independent of circumstance. At least, this is the vision of true freedom that resonates with me.

In order to arrive at such freedom, there must be a building up. Some might call it a discipline, or a practice. You build up a life, build trust, self-confidence, a healthy sense of ego, a community around yourself, and then at some point, you let it go. This letting go is both a "collapse" of the practice as well as the true fruition of practice. It's not that we push it away, but we let it go into a larger vision of freedom that allows us to live within the practice without identification with it.

There are many spiritual paths available today, from paganism, shamanism, new age-ism, established religions, and countless others. A worthwhile question to ask, I believe, is what distinguishes an *authentic* spiritual path from an inauthentic one?

What I've noted is that not all so-called "spiritual" paths follow the same trajectory, and yet, many do. The following trajectory is what I consider to be the arc of an authentic path: begin by building yourself up with love, with practice, through community and other such means. And then at some point, *there's a turn toward selflessness,* and it's this selflessness that I see as rooted in the capacity to allow for the whole thing to crumble, when it's time. Everything that you worked hard to build—admittedly around this project of self—you then let go of, and that's the true freedom of an authentic spiritual path. We build it up for the purpose of allowing it to give way to something larger. (As a side note, this trajectory also points to the important fact that we don't become selfless *before* building a healthy sense of self, or else it could easily devolve into codependency and/or martyrdom.)

We all experience hints of this in smaller ways. For example, we may work very hard for a long time on a project until we're done; then we just let it go. Without working hard to begin with, there's no real letting go, as there may be regret about having held back.

We want to live fully so that when it comes time for our death, we can let go fully. This was one of the contemplations on the first line on death. Similarly, we *build* a strong practice, so that it gives us a jumping off point when we're ready. It's not that we abandon our practice, but we let go of our prior "self-improvement" projects into the deeper and truer practice of selfless effort, which transforms our relationship to practice. From the outside, it may appear no different. We may still appear to be "practicing" on our cushion or chair, but who we are within that practice will have undergone a profound transformation.

Viewed in this way, a collapse of something we've built can be seen for what it truly is—an old life falling away to make room for the new, or a transformation. Without impermanence—that is, without the collapse of what we've built—we can't experience the freshness that comes with the rebirth of something new: a new project, a new path, a new identity, a new life. The contemplation of this particular line opens us up to letting go of what is decaying and moves us toward what wants to be born. Embracing the collapse is to embrace the birth of a new life.

Sometimes we resist the collapse. We hold onto the structure of our lives—whether it be in the form of a relationship, a job, even a practice—long after its "due date," as they say.

Earlier in my life, I was a doctoral student in mathematical modeling after obtaining a bachelor's and master's degree in mathematics. After two years of coursework, I had a series of medical issues that pulled me out of the grind of doctoral studies. When I returned to my studies, nothing was the same. I could no longer imagine devoting my working life to producing papers that maybe six to eight people in the world would understand or even care about.

Then I went to see an elder friend of mine named Chuck. I told him about my dilemma, how I couldn't imagine continuing on the path I was on, and yet, I had put so many years into it that I didn't want to let all that hard work go to waste. I said to him, "I don't want to flush the whole thing down the toilet."

Without missing a beat, he replied, "Hey Yuichi, have you considered the possibility that it's already gone down the toilet?"

Sometimes life is like this. The structure of our life has already collapsed, but we're the last to know. We tell ourselves that if we keep trying, we might preserve something of it, but it's already long gone! When Chuck said what he did, I felt the truth of his words which allowed me to accept what already was—my life had collapsed. It was up to me to notice it and begin charting a new course. And there was tremendous peace in that.

I subsequently withdrew from my studies, taught for a few years, became interested in another field through the teaching experience itself, obtained a doctorate in a field related to teaching rather than the more abstruse field of mathematical modeling, and became a tenured professor. And now I find myself letting that life go into a new one once again.

When my life as a doctoral student in mathematical modeling collapsed to ruins, I was slow to know. I had very little inkling of the impermanent nature of the things we build, including our lives, and I struggled through the transition longer than I likely needed to. But also, I didn't linger too long. I've seen better in terms of adaptability, and I've seen worse, both in others as well as in other areas of my life.

I'm reminded of a poem by Rumi called, "The three fish."

"The Three Fish" translated by Coleman Barks[26]

from *The Essential Rumi.* Harper Collins, 1995.

---

[26] Reprinted here with permission from the translator.

This is the story of the lake and the three big fish
that were in it, one of them intelligent,
another half-intelligent,
            and the third, stupid.

Some fishermen came to the edge of the lake
with their nets. The three fish saw them.
The intelligent fish decided at once to leave,
to make the long, difficult trip to the ocean.

He thought,
            "I won't consult with these two on this.
They will only weaken my resolve, because they love
this place so. They call it *home*. Their ignorance
will keep them here."

When you're traveling, ask a traveler for advice,
not someone whose lameness keeps him in one place.

Muhammad says,
            "Love of one's country
is part of the faith."
                        But don't take that literally!
Your real "country" is where you're heading,
not where you *are*.
Don't misread that *hadith*.

In the ritual ablutions, according to tradition,

_____

there's a separate prayer for each body part.
When you snuff water up your nose to cleanse it,
beg for the scent of the spirit. The proper prayer is,
"Lord, wash me. My hand has washed this part of
me,
but my hand can't wash my spirit.
            I can wash this skin,
but you must wash *me.*"

A certain man used to say the wrong prayer
for the wrong hole. He'd say the nose-prayer
when he splashed his behind. Can the odor of heaven
come from our rumps? Don't be humble with fools.
Don't take pride into the presence of a master.

It's right to love your home place, but first ask,
"Where is that, really?"

The wise fish saw the men and their nets and said,
"I'm leaving."

Ali was told a secret doctrine by Muhammad
and told not to tell it, so he whispered it down
the mouth of a well. Sometimes there's no one to talk
to>
You must just set out on your own.

So the intelligent fish made its whole length
a moving footprint and, like a deer the dogs chase,
suffered greatly on its way, but finally made it
to the edgeless safety of the sea.

The half-intelligent fish thought,
          "My guide
has gone. I ought to have gone with him,
but I didn't, and now I've lost my chance
to escape.
          I wish I'd gone with him."
Don't regret what's happened. If it's in the past,
let it go. Don't even *remember* it!

A certain man caught a bird in a trap.
The bird says, "Sir, you have eaten many cows and
sheep
in your life, and you're still hungry. The little bit
of meat on my bones won't satisfy you either.
If you let me go, I'll give you three pieces of wisdom.
One I'll say standing on your hand. One on your roof.
And one I'll speak from the limb of that tree."

The man was interested. He freed the bird and let it
stand
on his hand.
          "Number One: Do not believe an absurdity,
no matter who says it."

The bird flew and lit on the man's roof. "Number
Two:
Do not grieve over what is past. It's over.
Never regret what has happened."

"By the way," the bird continued, "in my body there's
a huge

pearl weighing as much as ten copper coins. It was meant
to be the inheritance of you and your children,
but now you've lost it. You could have owned
the largest pearl in existence, but evidently
it was not meant to be."

The man started wailing like a woman in childbirth.
The bird said: "Didn't I just say, *Don't grieve
for what's in the past?* And also: *Don't believe
an absurdity?* My entire body doesn't weight
as much as ten copper coins. How could I have
a pearl that heavy inside me?"

The man came to his senses. "All right.
Tell me Number Three."

"Yes. You've made such good use of the first two!"

Don't give advice to someone who's groggy
and falling asleep. Don't throw seeds on the sand.
Some torn places cannot be patched.

Back to the second fish,
            the half-intelligent one.
He mourns the absence of his guide for a while,
and then thinks, "What can I do to save myself
form these men and their nets? Perhaps if pretend
to be already dead!
            I'll belly up on the surface
and float like weeds float, just giving myself totally
to the water. To die before I die, as Muhammad

said to."
So he did that.

He bobbed up and down, helpless,
within arm's reach of the fishermen.

"Look at this! The best and biggest fish
is dead."
One of the men lifted him by the tail,
spat on him, and threw him up on the ground.

He rolled over and over and slid secretly near
the water, and then, back in.

Meanwhile,
the third fish, the dumb one, was agitatedly
jumping about, trying to escape with his agility
and cleverness.
The net, of course, finally closed
around him, and as he lay in the terrible
frying-pan bed, he thought,
"If I get out of this,
I'll never live again in the limits of a lake.
Next time, the ocean! I'll make
the infinite my home."

The fishermen with their nets are like the grim reaper
with his sickle. They signal the end of a life-stage,
the collapse of a life structure we have so dedicatedly

built. It is a time for acknowledging the end of one life-phase and transition into another, setting us ever closer to the ultimate goal of the infinite sea. If we hold on, trying to deny the transitory nature of the life we have built, we suffer like the third fish, or are hampered by doubt like the second fish, only to wiggle out from one stage to another after much pain and struggle.

Keeping impermanence at the forefront of our minds allows us to be more like the intelligent fish. We move toward our true home, maybe with a sense of grace and with less hesitation.

When we hold on too tightly to a job, a relationship, a lifestyle long past its collapse, and we finally let go, we often think, "Why was I holding on so tight all this time?" We hold on because of fear, because of our resistance to change, because of our attachment to security, or because of a longing for the past. Sometimes we hold on and we aren't even aware that we're doing so. When we undergo such painful transitions, we hope we can grow from the experience, namely that we can learn to let go earlier and embrace change more readily.

Some of us might say that we "learn things the hard way" or "when we're in enough pain, we'll make the change." But this is no different than believing ourselves to always act the part of the third fish. We *can* grow and learn. Maybe we won't transform into the first fish immediately, but to become even the second fish is growth for some of us.

The Course in Miracles says that we each have a curriculum we're here to learn—that is, a set of life lessons, if you will—and the only variable is time. We learn these lessons in a moment or in a lifetime. The choice as to whether we learn them now or in a lifetime is our free will. Not the lessons themselves.

One well-known way to shorten the time we muck about learning a lesson—i.e., shape-shifting from the third fish to the second, or from the second to the first—is through raising our awareness. With heightened awareness, our threshold for pain is lowered. What was once barely perceptible pain before becomes more acute, and with that, we move toward change sooner. Meditation, as well as other forms of spiritual practice, helps us to raise our awareness in such a manner.

Another way is to address our attachment to security, directly, through the contemplation of impermanence. When we truly see into the impermanent nature of all phenomena, including the various aspects of our lives that we work so hard to build, we can notice when things are ripening for change—that is, when a collapse is imminent—and in turn, we can let go before things become unnecessarily painful. We begin to recognize that it is our own clutching and clinging that causes much of the pain during these periods of transition. In letting go when truly called for, and not months or even years after the fact, we can move through our lives with greater grace and ease. This is one of the gifts of contemplating and embracing impermanence.

Reification

Reification is the process of making something (usually abstract) more concrete or solid, such as into an object. For example, friendship is a reification. In reality, there's no such *thing* as a friendship. There are two people who might enjoy spending time together, telling jokes, eating food, going on trips and the like, but the *idea* of friendship is nothing more than a label or concept put upon these people who are interacting in a particular way. We've turned a way of interacting among two people into something solid called friendship. The same can be said for relationships. It is again a conceptual overlay upon people who interact with one another in a particular manner.

Similarly, if we gather a group of people and have them trade and barter goods, maybe even come up with a form of currency to expedite the bartering process, we would call this an economy. In this manner, "economy" is a reification. It's a conceptual imputation upon people who behave a certain way.

In the same vein, democracy is a reification. No such thing actually exists. It's simply a concept. Interestingly, many people are willing to give their lives over for a reification, a solidified concept such as democracy.

Also, when we judge others or ourselves, what we're really doing is reifying in our minds. For example, if I call someone a jerk, that's a reification, a solidification. In reality, it's simply that the person is talking or acting in a certain manner, but I'm choosing to put the label of "jerk" on that person, someone who is ever-changing and could be saving someone else's life in another moment.

Just to be clear, reification doesn't mean that one is applying a false concept, such as what many harsh judgments of others are. It simply means to turn something solid or concrete, whether it's correct or not. It points to the act of making a conceptual overlay upon a *dynamic* phenomenon.

We can also apply this term to actual physical objects, such as a home. A home can be considered a reification of an architect's vision. An architect may imagine and dream up a home, and reify it as a blueprint. The blueprint then is a reification of his thinking and envisioning, used by carpenters to then build the house.

School teachers will sit down to think about a lesson, and so the lesson plan is a reification of that thinking process. From that lesson plan, a teacher will teach, and students will form concepts in their mind around the topic at hand, and these concepts that are formed are then reifications in the students' minds.[27]

In Dharma—or if you think about it, most spirituality—the concern is with *experience* itself, such as the experience of breathing, walking, perceiving, or simply being. And course, there are the variety of spiritual *experiences* that many of us undergo throughout our lives. Experience is intrinsically flowing and fluid. And yet, when we reify an experience in some way, we more or less freeze it in time; we take away the fluidity of experience itself, and thereby, take a step away from it. One might even say that we lose the essence of experience through reification. Christian mystics sometimes say that whatever *concept* you have of God, it is already off because it's nothing more than a concept, while God is not a sterile concept. That is, as soon as you have a concept of an experience or perception, it's no longer the original experience or perception itself.

In spirituality, it's generally the spiritual experience itself, and not the concept, that transforms, connects, and opens. Oftentimes, it's our own conceptualizations, whether of God or spirituality, that actually impede our genuine experience of it.

---

[27] This iterative cycle between reification and process (or participation) has been written about quite eloquently by the sociologist Etienne Wenger in his book *Communities of Practice: Learning, Meaning, and Identity.*

In Dharma, the most central reification at hand is the thing we call *self.* It's taught that we mentally create this concept called self, and because it's something *built* in our minds, it too is bound to collapse. In fact, the genuine collapse of the conceptual self can stand as a synonym for enlightenment.

When we examine our bodies—whether by looking down or in the mirror—we see a body. Few of us would say that our true essence is our body. So we might consider our thoughts, but if we've engaged in some meditation, we quickly see that thoughts come and go, and it becomes difficult to identify ourselves with them after a while. Instead, we begin to view our thoughts in the same way we might view scenery from a car or a train. They're passing phenomena. The same goes for feelings and emotions.

From a pragmatic point of view, identifying ourselves as our thoughts or feelings isn't the most conducive toward peace or happiness. If I believe that I am my thoughts, then each "bad" thought brings about some measure of shame, and similarly, each "good" thought brings about pride. But thoughts themselves can't be controlled, and soon, I'll likely feel out of control. The same with feelings. If I identify myself as my feelings, then my life becomes a roller-coaster ride. When my feelings are bad and depressed, then I'm a "depressed person" rather than someone who temporarily feels depressed. The former loses perspective that would help in carrying onward. In fact, the slight dis-identification, not suppression, of emotions can support the acceptance and processing of those emotions.

So if not our bodies, our thoughts, or our feelings, what then? Maybe there's consciousness or awareness itself?[28] Some practitioners have found tremendous freedom in identifying with awareness— sometimes called the "witness" consciousness—rather than thoughts and feelings because it frees one from identifying with the ever-shifting, often tumultuous nature of thoughts and feelings. I, too, have found great benefit in this shift from thoughts to feelings to awareness, in my own practice.

And yet, even awareness is fleeting. During more extended meditation retreats, it's not uncommon for a practitioner to notice the arising and fading of consciousness or awareness itself. In other words, it too isn't constant or permanent, for it depends upon having an object, whether sensory or mental in nature. That is, it lacks an independently-existing intrinsic nature that we might call a self.

One of the primary teachings of the Buddha is that no matter how far down we look, we won't find (in any empirical sense) a permanent, lasting, intrinsic self. We might impute a concept of self upon tempo-

---

[28] I recognize that I'm conflating two words that for some are not used interchangeably. To be more precise, I'm using them both to stand for consciousness as described in the *Abhidharma*.

rary configurations of form, perception, consciousness, and the like, but that is only a reification. Just as we cannot empirically find any such *thing* called relationship, friendship, economy, or democracy, we'll be hard-pressed to find an actual entity called a self.

Certainly there is a body that comes and goes, but where does this self begin and end, especially when it is constantly shedding used cells and producing new ones? And if the body dies, or parts of it are lopped off, what happens to the self? Is the self simply the brain or the heart? In this manner, we can go through each aspect of what we think we are, from the form (i.e., body) to our feelings, our perceptions, our mental formations, and our consciousness, and see that each is impermanent and lacking an intrinsic, independent existence as a self.

These different *aspects* of what we often consider the "self"—i.e., form, feelings, perceptions, mental formations, and consciousness—are referred to as the five aggregates or *skandhas*. Much of Buddhist practice consists of seeing through their impermanent and non-solid nature. *It's taught that our clinging to one or more of these, which results from identification with them as our "self," is the cause of our suffering.* On the other hand, to see through their non-solid nature and to recognize that they fail to form a basis for self is to realize profound freedom.

Reactions to Non-Self

He who replies to words of Doubt
Doth put the Light of Knowledge out…
  —from "Auguries of Innocence" by William Blake

Upon hearing teachings on *anatta* (non-self), people usually have one of two reactions. One is that of relief or even elation, that we needn't make such a big deal out of the self and all of its projects since it's a mere fabrication or delusion! On the other hand, some take it hard. It can feel nihilistic. "What's the point then?" becomes the reaction. Or else those with certain spiritual but non-Buddhist backgrounds might wonder, "Does that mean we have no soul?"

Because of how common these reactions seem to be, I want to address these concerns.

It's said that there are a number of primary fears a practitioner might experience. One of the most common is in reaction to the teachings on emptiness, of which the teachings on non-self can be construed as a sub-segment. It *should* feel frightening to the ego, as it means the utter extinguishing of it, since ego is nothing more than the after-effect of reifying a belief in this permanent self.

Sometimes this kind of fear is masked by an intellectualization of the fear itself. Instead of directly experiencing the fear and working with it on that level, some of us "go into our heads" and pose questions borne of this fear and doubt. I would suggest that questions such as "What's the point then?" or "Does that mean we have no soul?" are actually such questions that mask a subtle fear-laden reaction to the teachings on non-self. In other words, rather than attempting to answer such questions directly—which might dim the light of true wisdom, as hinted at by Blake—it can sometimes be more helpful to listen to what's underneath the question. [29] If we can get at the fearful or aversive reaction to the teachings on non-self that may lie underneath our questions, then in turn, we would do well to be gentle with ourselves. We needn't push ahead with the non-self agenda, but simply hold it as a possibility that may grow in us with time.

---

[29] For example, consider when a student in a math class asks, "What's the point of studying this?" A teacher can respond by listing out all the virtues of studying mathematics, but this is rarely satisfying for the student. If the teacher listens more carefully to what's being expressed *underneath* the question, she might hear a complaint along the lines of, "This experience that I'm being put through in math class doesn't connect for me. It has no intrinsic value for me." If the teacher can hear those whisperings beneath the original question, then that teacher can begin to consider how to change the curriculum and his/her approach to teaching itself, so students can feel more connected to the experience of learning mathematics. This would likely lead to a more satisfying conclusion for all concerned. I've taken this illustrative example from the writings of mathematics educator, Brent Davis.

It may also be helpful to examine life experiences when the sense of self, or even self-consciousness, was thinned out, and see if there wasn't an accompanying sense of freedom in that. Perhaps it happened while dancing or maybe in falling in love? Sometimes when we're listening to someone whose suffering dwarves our own, we "get out of ourselves," that is, our sense of self thins out. It's this freedom from our usually strong sense of self that is the gift of acknowledging and/or embracing the truth of non-self, which can make the teachings more palatable.

From this perspective—that of cherishing the sense of freedom inherent in the teachings on non-self—one might notice how much of our suffering comes from having a fixed and somber seriousness around our own projects of self. Or we might see it in others. The more we loosen around our own sense of self, the more we might recognize how others suffer from clinging, without question, to self and the self's agenda.

So the point then, is this: the more we can recognize the non-essential nature of self, the more informed our concern and compassion can be for ourselves and others. We begin to recognize that much of our suffering is derived primarily from believing in permanence where there is only impermanence, and in something substantial called a self when there is only the concept of it. This isn't to say that we then just dump the teachings of impermanence and non-self onto others. Instead, we see more clearly into the nature and cause of suffering within ourselves as well as those around us, and recognize that the more that we're able to live in an open state while embracing the impermanence and non-self or empty nature of this life, the more others around us can relax into that as well, even without us saying a word about it.

Stated from a more Christian-like perspective, we lose ourselves so that we might be of greater use to others. We become a more open and pure "vessel" of God, if you will. I liken it to the attitude expressed by St. Francis of Assisi in his famous prayer:

Lord, make me an instrument of thy peace!
That where there is hatred, I may bring love.
That where there is wrong, I may bring the spirit of
forgiveness.
That where there is discord, I may bring harmony.
That where there is error, I may bring truth.
That where there is doubt, I may bring faith.
That where there is despair, I may bring hope.
That where there are shadows, I may bring light.
That where there is sadness, I may bring joy.
Lord, grant that I may seek rather to comfort, than to
be comforted.
To understand, than to be understood.
To love, than to be loved.
For it is by self-forgetting that one finds.
It is by forgiving that one is forgiven.
It is by dying that one awakens to Eternal Life.

What I find striking about the prayer is the utter lack of self-concern. He doesn't wonder to himself, "Do I have a soul?" (which is very similar to the Buddha, who also did not entertain questions of whether we have souls or not). For St. Francis, genuine meaning, fulfillment, and freedom exist in moving toward the actualization of non-self, or what he calls "self-forgetting." (The Buddha qualified his choice not to respond to questions on the existence of a soul by adding that his concern was primarily for our liberation, not our intellectual comfort or amusement.)

It can be striking to encounter someone who embodies this selfless quality. When I first met one of my teachers in this life, my experience of him was profoundly different than all of my personal encounters up until that point. It was as if there was no self operating behind his personality. He was fully present to me, and yet, I didn't feel this constant agenda being put upon me, which I had grown so used to up to that point. I remember writing in my journal, "A man of truth is a man who is not there," which is awkward in phrasing and imagery, but gets at something close to this idea of someone whose sense of self has been thinned out, someone who lives close to the reality of *anatta,* as taught by the Buddha.

And this is in stark contrast to those we might reify (!) as being egotistical. Usually, such persons strike us as being full of a solid sense of self with its various projects and agendas. When viewed from the perspective of the teachings on non-self, we might notice how much compounding and fabricating of concept upon concept is occurring in such a personality! We might begin to understand why we don't feel free and open around such persons, and why compassion might be the natural response to such a solidified personality.

Vipassana

These teachings on *anatta* ("non-self") are part of a larger teaching on the three characteristics that mark the existence of all sentient beings: *anicca* (impermanence), *dukkha* (suffering or dissatisfaction), and *anatta* (non-self). In a form of meditation called *Vipassana* (translated as "clear seeing"), we examine our bodily sensations, emotions, and thoughts in light of these three characteristics. In other words, when bodily sensations arise, for example, we note the sensations while also observing their impermanent, unsatisfactory, and non-solid nature. We do the same with thoughts and feelings. In time, this method of meditation helps us loosen our clinging to false hopes, unrealistic expectations, misguided pursuits, and generally, delusional thinking.

The line at hand ("What is built is impermanent and is bound to collapse") then, can be the springboard to contemplations on the impermanent nature of things, civilizations, practices themselves, and ultimately, of the reification we call self. When applied to self, the meditations harken back to the contemplations on death, but not just the death of the body, but of what might be called our psychological self.

As we learn to let go of various aspects of "self," it's like the snake shedding its old skin. Most of us have known the experience of letting go of one way of living so that we can begin another. Whatever self it was that constituted the older life dies into a new self. We could say that part of our identity dies during this transition, but a question worth pondering is this: where did the old self go when it "died?"

Whereas with physical death or the shedding of our skin, there is the actual physical remnant of our old self, what happens when we experience a psychological death? Where does that old self go? It simply disappears, right? That past self might as well have been a dream. It almost doesn't feel real. And in that, we gain a glimmer of the reified nature of that self, that it was merely an imputation—something built and collapsed, like a wave that during its crest, we called a self. It was a concept. An idea.

Preliminary:
1. Set time and place.
2. Relaxed and upright posture; allow for some settling.

Beginning:
3. Refuge.
4. Bodhicitta.

Middle:
5. Set timer to **six minutes** and practice shamatha
   for those six minutes.
6. Re-set the timer to **twelve minutes,** and use the
   line *"Whatever is built is impermanent and is
   bound to collapse"* as the basis for contemplation
   and consider these questions. (You might try
   each or any one of them.)

   a) Contemplate the impermanent nature of your
      creative or artistic pursuits. If you're some-
      one who creates paintings, poems, music, fur-
      niture, and so on, use these objects in your

contemplations. If not, you might consider the way you live your daily life—that is, the structure of your life—as the object of your contemplation. As you hold whatever it is in mind, ask yourself, "Do I in any way hold these things to be lasting or permanent? Is there a part of me that wishes for them to last without collapse of some kind? Am I willing to see that whether it is a work of art or a life-style, it could become dated and old in time?" The idea is to look for ways in which we hold onto the desire for lasting value in things that are bound to lose such value.

b) Contemplate your relationship to status and fame. Or you might expand your contemplation to the eight worldly winds and ask, "How much do I cling to my sense of status (or whatever worldly wind you are contemplating)? Can I recognize that it is bound to change and collapse in one way or another? Can I imagine a life that isn't in pursuit of these, but is shaped instead by spiritual principles? What might some of those principles be?" Also, "How much am I motivated by a desire to avoid disrepute (or whatever worldly wind that's paired with the one you contemplated from above)? Can I see where my aversion for that may have cut short a richer experience in life? Can I imagine softening my aversion for it? Again, can I imagine shaping a life based upon spiritual principles rather than my attachments and aversions, in short, my preferences?"

c) Contemplate your relationship to your spiritual practice, whatever it may be. Some questions to consider are, "Do I cling to my practice as if my identity were derived from it? Can I see how that kind of tightness of mind might be counter to my true intent in practicing? Or am I too loose in building a practice? Do I need to tell people about my spiritual practice? If so, why might that be?" Further questions include, "How much of my spiritual practice feels like a cocoon to rest in, and how much of it feels like a springboard into selflessness? (Both may be important depending upon one's current life state.) Does this balance feel right for now? Can I find a way to bring my practice more fully into my daily life, or does it feel as if I have two compartmentalized lives going on, one during meditation, and then the rest of my life?" In general, "Can I see that my spiritual practice is a valuable asset I am building that I may one day also outgrow or reshape into something new, meaning that it will likely collapse in its current form? Am I at ease with this idea?"

d) Examine the ways in which you reify people in your life through judgments. Similarly, examine how you do this to yourself. Can you

see how these judgments are mental construc-
tions that freeze a dynamic *process* called a
human being? What are your most common
reifications in these regards? Put differently,
what are the stories you tell about yourself *to
yourself?* Can you see through them as reifications? Can you imagine slowly letting
them go? What would happen if you
did? What would you be left with? What
would happen to others and to you if your reifications (stories) of others and yourself became thinner and thinner? Can you allow for
a collapse of all that you believe?

Toward the end of the time, relax into the state of being that reflecting produces in you.   We're aiming
for about **18 total minutes of practice time**!

Ending:
7.   Offer merit.

Chapter 17: The impermanence of that which arises

Here's the fifth line: *Whatever rises up is impermanent and is bound to fall down.*

Clearly, many of the comments from the last chapter could apply to this line, such as buildings and bridges, civilizations, as well as status and reputation. Also, this line speaks to the impermanence of our emotions, which rise and fade.

An important Dharma teaching that ties into this line is the teaching on dependent origination, or dependent *arising*. One of the more illustrative ways this can be explained is to think of a wood fire. When we examine the fire, we can say that it is dependent upon a host of causes and conditions that support its existence. For example, the wood itself is one of the conditions required for this particular fire to exist. We also need air to keep the fire going. Someone or something had to have lit the fire—that is, there had to be a spark of some kind to set the fire in motion. The existence of this fire, we say then, is dependent upon these various causes and conditions, and if one of these conditions were to be removed—for example, if one could suck all of the air out of the space—the fire would cease to exist. It would be the same if someone were to remove the wood, unless we were to supply some other source of fuel.

This is a common metaphor given in the suttas on what a sentient being (or the five aggregates that constitute a sentient being) essentially is. And enlightenment, or *nirvana* (meaning to "blow out"), is described then as the extinguishing of the three poisons (ignorance, attachment, and aversion) through removal of the causes and conditions that support the existence of the five aggregates. So when the causes and conditions for the existence of the five aggregates are removed, that sentient being is said to escape the cycle of birth and rebirth.

This is to say that enlightenment is possible precisely because of impermanence. Because what arises can fall away, the five aggregates can also fade away.

The teachings on dependent arising also help us to better understand the concept of emptiness. Let's go back to the fire metaphor. There's no aspect of the fire—not even the tiniest part of it—that exists *independent* of the causes and conditions. In other words, we cannot isolate a part of the fire that will continue existing when we remove the air, the wood, and so on. Another way to say this is that we cannot isolate some part of the fire that existed *prior* to the causes and conditions coming together, or *long after* they have been removed.

We describe this as saying that there is no part of the fire that has independent existence. Its whole existence, in fact, is dependent upon the causes and conditions being there.

When Buddhists speak of emptiness, they mean exactly the same thing. There is no independent thing called fire, *outside of the causes and conditions*; when these causes and conditions are removed, the fire ceases to exist entirely. We say that the fire has no core "self" or independently-existing, intrinsic self "on the inside." It is just an appearance of something we happen to call "fire" whose temporary existence rests on a whole web of other things that are also temporary, also without a core "self" on the inside.

One might liken the entire interplay of phenomena to the play of light and shadows, which in itself would be a wondrous display to behold, only that some parts of this play of light (namely, us) begin to assert independent existence and in turn must suffer through all that comes with that assertion (or forgetting)!

In the Dharma, it's taught that all phenomena are empty (of a core self), dependent upon causes and conditions that constitute their existence, and cease to exist in that particular form when these causes and conditions are removed. Again, there is no independently-existing, intrinsic self on the inside. And specifically, this is applied to us, to sentient beings. We may impute some essential being or self to ourselves and others, but that would be merely a projection onto, or conceptualization of, a dynamic process or experience that we call "self."

In this manner, these teachings on dependent arising form a wonderful bridge between the teachings on impermanence to emptiness. When we truly see the impermanence of all phenomena, and we connect that with the idea that all things are upheld in seeming existence by the causes and conditions which are impermanent themselves, we then gain a genuine glimpse into *emptiness*.

Emptiness doesn't mean that everything is simply nothing, but rather that if one looks carefully for the core or essence of any thing or person, one will be hard-pressed to find any such essence that is permanently enduring and independent of other things and persons. A truer vision is to see the whole thing (of which each of us is just one tiny, ever-changing, momentary speck) as one interconnected, ever-shifting web of *interactions*.

It's this large web of interpenetrating interactions, sometimes referred to as "Indra's net," that's said to mark the true appearance of phenomenal reality. The momentary crystallization or solidification of form, feeling, perception, volition, and mental consciousness is just that—a momentary configuration of an ever-dynamic play of light.

Afflictive Emotions

When it comes to our emotions and mental states, there are certain causes and conditions that give rise to positive states, and others that give rise to negative ones, usually referred to as afflictive emotions. For example, if we feel angry, there are specific causes and conditions for that to have arisen. But this is good news, since everything that arises must fall away!

These teachings on dependent arising are a profoundly hopeful set of teachings. In my 20's when I would get depressed, a regular accompanying thought I had was, "I'm always going to be depressed." Had I known the teachings on impermanence, they would have offered a ray of hope— dependent upon how deeply they had penetrated my mind.

Not only that, had someone pointed out to me that my mental state was upheld by certain causes and conditions, and that with the removal of those causes and conditions, my mental state would not be able to continue, I would have felt tremendous hope as well as enthusiasm for practice. In a sense, that *is* my life story. I've been practicing across decades to slowly extricate myself from suffering in one way or another. This *is* the promise of Dharma practice—freedom from suffering.

As I previously mentioned, it's taught that our suffering arises due to our attachment or clinging, much of which occurs based upon a misperception of the true nature of things, or a belief in permanence where there is no permanence, independent existence where there is no independent existence. Much of our practice in the Dharma then, is examining where we're attached, how we're attached, and learning how to let go a little bit better through a closer examination of reality. As we learn to let go a bit more, we cling less, and this in turn reduces the related host of causes and conditions that give rise to suffering and the afflictive emotions.

The contemplation of impermanence is considered one of the primary tools for lessening our attachments and clinging, whether to sensual pleasures, to seeking out security where there is none, or to our sense of self. There are other tools worth exploring, but one can do a lot worse than contemplating impermanence and death.

The verse concludes with two more lines:

So also, friendship and enmity, fortune and sorrow,
good and evil,
all the thoughts that run through one's mind—every-
thing is always changing.

These final two lines are a summary statement of the preceding lines we've been exploring. It's generally taught that being able to hold both friends and supposed enemies alike, equanimously, is the basis for true compassion. A major hurdle in the development of genuine and great compassion is our clinging to the categories of "friend" and "not friend." In seeing through the impermanent nature of such categories, we might loosen our clinging to them, and in turn, move closer to a universal love toward others.

It's similar with fortune and sorrow, good and evil, as well as any other mental categorizations placed upon our experience. When we hold on to such labels as somehow having a permanent feature—or an ontological truthfulness, despite being nothing more than a reification—we lose touch with the ever-shifting, dynamic nature of reality, and in turn, our capacity for moving joyfully, gracefully, and effortlessly along with change is diminished.

—Week twelve: Our last week together

Preliminary:
1. Set time and place.
2. Relaxed and upright posture; allow for some settling.

Beginning:
3. Refuge.
4. Bodhicitta.

Middle:
5. Set timer to **seven minutes** and practice shamatha for those seven minutes.
6. Re-set the timer to **fourteen minutes,** and engage in any of the following contemplative exercises, or some combination. (Basically we're upping the practice to 21 total minutes, broken down into thirds.)

Use the line *"Whatever rises up is impermanent and is bound to fall down"* as the basis for contemplation and consider these questions. (You might try each of them.)

a) Contemplate the teachings on dependent arising. You might re-read the passage on it, or
search the internet and see if there is a description of it that resonates for you. Can you
grasp how it logically leads to the lack of an
intrinsic, independent "self?"

b) Consider the arising of any afflictive emotions or mental states—usually categorized
into the five primary afflictive emotions of
denial (or confusion), aggression (or anger),
pride (or defensiveness or even victim-hood),
clinging (or expectations), and jealousy (or
competitiveness). Working with these afflictive states could be the basis for an entire vol-
ume of books! ☺ But for now, you can
simply *contemplate* their impermanent nature. You might note that no emotional state
has persisted across your life, without
change. If you currently suffer from one or
more, you might note that with open awareness upon them, these state are impermanent
from moment to moment. Although you may
feel rather miserable throughout the self-ex-
amination, the texture and tone of the state
actually shifts each moment. If you can notice the impermanent nature of these feelings,
you may even begin to notice some sense of
space around them.

Next try to entwine your understanding of dependent origination upon your afflictive state. You might gain a glimpse of the unsolid nature of your state, that there is no solid thing called anger, or sadness, or loneliness, or depression, and so on. It's both impermanent and unsolid. These contemplations, as mentioned before, form the basis for Vipassana meditation, and can help to greatly loosen and lighten the heaviness and denseness around and within some of these emotions.

Toward the end of the time, relax into the state of being that your reflection produces in you.

Ending:
7. Offer merit.

Chapter 18: Conclusion— Putting the whole container of practice together

I've talked about emptiness in a number of ways. There is yet another way of thinking about it, which is to consider this reality as a kind of dream or mirage, or temporary and illusory in nature. I have a friend who refers to it more as being like a hologram. To help us with this in our practice, we can use a simple phrase, "Like a dream," as in "This reality is like a dream."

In the first few chapters of this book, I mentioned the idea of a practice "container" with a beginning, middle, and end. The *beginning* of this container starts with "refuge," which I described as touching into something deeper, larger, or even divine or sacred, whether within oneself or without. This is followed by invoking the altruistic intention of bodhicitta, intended to be included into our motivations, that of compassion for others, and out of that compassion, a recognition that moving toward enlightenment will afford us the capacity for greater effect upon others. We seek out qualities of greater clarity, openness, and happiness, not for the sheer purpose of being clear, open, and happy, but so that we can be of greater benefit to others. Refuge and bodhicitta, in short, constitute the beginning or front end of our practice "container." The *ending* is offering merit— that whatever good or value arising from our practice is offered for the benefit of others. And so this is what we do.

But there is also the *middle*. The key point in the middle is to practice whatever form of meditation we do in a way that avoids making things more solid and stuck, anchored around self and self's projects. What we don't want to do is sit there thinking, "*I'm* practicing. *I'm* the one meditating, and this is *my* thing..." and so on and so forth. Instead, we want to practice with a light quality so things open up, both the practice and ourselves.

One way to support this lightening of our practice is to recite a simple phrase—"like a dream"—during our practice. We pause to take notice or take stock of what is around and within us, and we gently say to ourselves, "like a dream." What we mean implicitly by this phrase is, "This existence that I believe to be real, these thoughts and emotions that also feel real, even this practice that may feel like the only real thing in my life—they are all like a dream, a loose fabrication of light and energy that appears solid and yet is translucent upon closer inspection."

One could use any phrase that points to a transient, evanescent phenomenon. For example, one could say, "Like a firefly." So the next time you're in the throes of infatuated love or in the midst of the most blissful meditative experience, you could say, "Like a firefly. Burns up for a while, lights things up, then it dies, like all things." Or you could say, "Like a cloud." Look around while in meditation, at a table for example, and say, "Like a cloud. This too will disperse in time as if it were never here."

Using phrases such as "Like a dream" helps to keep our practice relaxed by keeping our minds more spacious and open. One could say that this is the pragmatic point of the teachings on dependent origination and emptiness. It's to say that this whole thing is like a dream, so try and relax. There's no point making a big deal about things because what we call reality is much more vast, mysterious, and illusory than most of us can imagine.

In this way, we enter our practice by touching into something greater than self through refuge, and we include others through raising an altruistic intention behind the practice. So again, it's not just a project of the self that we undertake. Then throughout the practice—at a pace that feels comfortable, such as every minute, or every five minutes, or even just once—we say to ourselves, "like a dream." When we say it and have a sensation or awareness of things loosening, we briefly stay with that awareness of "It's not as solid as it usually seems to be."

We practice in this manner until the end, when we dedicate the merit, again, in order to keep our practice unburdened of the ego's agenda as much as possible. In this way, our practice doesn't get wound tightly around the self, and instead can stay relaxed and open. When we keep our practice relaxed, it stands a better chance of sustaining itself.

Now we've brought together the whole of the container with its three parts: the excellent beginning, excellent middle, and excellent end. This is the practice moving forward.

In closing, I wish you well in sustaining your practice from this point forward. If you connected with any of the contemplations, I encourage you to stay with them for however long they offer benefit, and sometimes, even when they don't *appear* to be helping; it's then that they may be doing their work underneath your notice. More than anything, my hope for you is that you show up to your practice on a regular basis. If you a miss a day or two, try not to make a big deal of it. It's only when you go a week or more without practicing that you might consider re-reading parts of this book to see what might be missing. There's a lot to digest here. Even if you sit daily, I believe there's value in reviewing many of the ideas in this book.

If you find yourself not practicing, another tactic is to vary your practice. One of my teachers says, "The best practice is the one you do." Whatever helps you show up to your practice is likely what's best for now (maybe it's chanting, dancing, walking meditation, visualization, and so on). And from there, perhaps you can trust your meditation practice to have its own self-correcting nature. If you keep showing up, attentive to what arises, you might find yourself deepening into the true nature of reality and into your practice. But try not to push too hard either. A relaxed and steady approach is best.

If you have further questions, I hope you feel free to contact me through email at yhanda@gmail.com. I can't predict the number of questions, but if they become overwhelming, I may choose to aggregate my responses in a blog. I can also be consulted as a meditation and/or life coach, if that is of interest to you. I can be found at www.yuichihanda.com. In the meantime, I wish you well in your practice and in your life, and may our paths cross again in the future. God bless, *metta*, and *om mani padme hung*.

Contemplative Meditation: How to Build a Sustainable Daily Practice

Disclaimer: The information provided herein is for educational and informational purposes only and solely as a self-help tool for your own use. Always seek the advice of your own Medical Provider and/or Mental Health Provider regarding any questions or concerns you have about your specific health or any medications, herbs or supplements you are currently taking and before implementing any recommendations or suggestions from any outside source. Do not disregard medical advice or delay seeking medical advice if necessary. This book is not intended as a substitute for the medical advice of physicians. Do not start or stop taking any medications without speaking to your own Medical Provider or Mental Health Provider. If you have or suspect that you have a medical or mental health problem, contact your own Medical Provider or Mental Health Provider promptly. Although the author and publisher have made every effort to ensure that the information in this book was correct at press time, the author and publisher do not assume and hereby disclaim any liability to any party for any loss, damage, or disruption caused by errors or omissions, whether such errors or omissions result from negligence, accident, or any other cause.

About Yuichi Handa

Yuichi likes to use this one picture over and over in his books and on Facebook. He needs someone to take more photos of him so that he has other versions of himself to show people.